SEEDS OF FAITH

Practices to Grow a Healthy Spiritual Life

J E R E M Y   L A N G F O R D

PARACLETE PRESS
BREWSTER, MASSACHUSETTS

Dedication

For my children—Tyler Joseph, Caitlin Marie, and Colin Daniel

---

Seeds of Faith: Practices to Grow a Healthy Spiritual Life

2009 Second Printing
2007 First Printing

Copyright © 2007 by Jeremy Langford

ISBN: 978-1-55725-439-9

Library of Congress Cataloging-in-Publication Data

Langford, Jeremy.
  Seeds of faith : practices to grow a healthy spiritual life / Jeremy Langford.
    p. cm.
  Includes bibliographical references.
  ISBN 978-1-55725-439-9
  1. Spiritual life--Catholic Church. I. Title.

  BX2350.3.L36 2007
  248.4'82--dc22

                                    2007047277

10 9 8 7 6 5 4 3 2

Published by Paraclete Press
Brewster, Massachusetts
www.paracletepress.com
Printed in the United States of America

Contents

INTRODUCTION **SEEDS OF FAITH**

Every moment and every event of every man's life on earth plants something in his soul. For just as the wind carries thousands of winged seeds, so each moment brings with it germs of spiritual vitality that come to rest imperceptibly in the minds and wills of men. Most of these unnumbered seeds perish and are lost, because men are not prepared to receive them: for such seeds as these cannot spring up anywhere except in the good soil of freedom, spontaneity and love.

—Thomas Merton

If you're reading this line, you're at least intrigued by the title of this book. Perhaps you're a seasoned seeker who recognizes echoes of Thomas Merton's classic book *New Seeds of Contemplation* and you wonder what's in store for you here. Or, maybe you're just beginning to nurture your spiritual life and are looking for reflections and practices that will help you on your way. Wherever you are on your faith journey—welcome. I hope you find this book a useful companion.

Let me say up front that this book is not about gardening or written for gardeners. Nor is it a how-to guide for living a spiritual life.

Rather, it draws on gardening as a metaphor to explore how God works in our lives. As Merton's quote above suggests, God is like a gardener who uses every moment and every event to plant something of spiritual significance in our lives. The better prepared we are to receive these "seeds of faith" and help them grow in our lives, the more we come to know God's love, to accept ourselves for who we are, to love others, and to enjoy the gift of life. And, in turn, the better able we are to share the seeds and fruits of faith with others. This book offers reflections and practices that help us prepare the soil of our lives to receive and nurture God's seeds of faith.

The Sower and the Seeds of Faith

The concept of God as a gardener is nothing new. The book of Genesis tells us that God "planted a garden in Eden," and strolled through creation "at the time of the evening breeze." Later in the Bible, the Gospel of Matthew includes a parable that portrays God as a sower who spreads the seeds of the Word far and wide in the hopes that they will take root in our lives.

This parable of the sower and the seed provides a helpful metaphor for understanding God and our response to God in the life of faith. And because it provides the structure of this book, I invite you to read and reflect on it using a practice that you can apply to each chapter of this book:

———————

◼ *Take a moment to gather yourself. Even if you're reading these words on the bus or in a noisy coffee shop, try to quiet your inner world.*

◼ *Clear your mind of to-do lists and worries. Remind yourself that you are in God's presence.*

◼ *Read through the selected passage slowly, paying careful attention to images, feelings, and thoughts that come to mind.*

◼ *If you are able, underline or write down in a notebook words and concepts that strike you; otherwise, try to hold them in your memory.*

◼ *When you finish reading the passage, pause—closing your eyes if you find that helpful—and reflect on what the words and entire passage mean to you, your personal history, your faith.*

◼ *Remember: This exercise is not about simply completing a task. The point is to recognize God's Word and your response to it. Ask God for the grace to be receptive to insight and meaning. Share your thoughts and feelings with God.*

◼ *Close with a prayer, such as the Our Father.*

Now, begin your reading of the parable of the sower and the seed:

That same day Jesus went out of the house and sat beside the sea. Such great crowds gathered around him that he got into a boat and sat there, while the whole crowd stood on the beach. And he told them many things in parables saying: "Listen! A sower went out to sow. And as he sowed, some seeds fell on the path, and the birds came and ate them up. Other seeds fell on the rocky ground, where they did not have much soil, and they sprang up quickly, since they had no depth of soil. But when the sun rose, they were scorched; and since they had no root, they withered away. Other seeds fell among thorns, and the thorns grew up and choked them. Other seeds fell on good soil and brought forth grain, some a hundredfold, some sixty, some thirty. Let anyone with ears listen!

Rich in metaphor and meaning, this parable raises many questions:

- *Who is the sower?*
- *What kind of seeds did he sow?*
- *Why did so many of the seeds fall on infertile earth?*
- *What qualifies as fertile soil?*
- *What was the yield, and how significant is a hundredfold yield?*
- *How can we "hear" and interpret this story for our own lives and spiritual practice?*

Like us, the disciples want to know why Jesus speaks in parables. Jesus explains, "The reason I speak to them in parables is that 'seeing they do not perceive, and hearing they do not listen, nor do they understand.'" In other words, Jesus wants us to lean in and listen hard to what he is trying to teach us about God and ourselves. The practices in this book are meant to help us have eyes to see and ears to hear God at work in our lives.

In his explanation of the parable, Jesus reveals that God is the sower, the Word is the seed, and we are the different types of soil. We're like the footpath if we hear the Word, but don't understand it and allow the evil one to snatch it away. We're like the rocky ground if we receive the Word with initial enthusiasm, but fail to let it take root in our lives, especially in times of trial, and thus allow it to die. We're like the thorny ground if we hear the Word, but let the cares of the world and the lure of personal gain choke it out. Finally, we're like the fertile soil if we hear the Word, understand it, and let it take root in our lives such that it bears fruit and yields a thirtyfold, sixtyfold, or hundredfold.

We can look at this parable from a different vantage point by asking: What if *we* are the seed? What if God sows us into the world?

If so, other questions arise:
- *What kind of seed are we, and what kind should we be?*
- *If we could choose, which type of soil would we land on?*
- *How well do we understand God the Gardener's plan for us?*
- *How do we fit into the larger garden of creation?*
- *What does the yield of our lives look like?*
- *Do we help other seeds in the garden grow, or do we choke them out?*

The purpose of this book is to transform these questions into practices that help us live our faith in nurturing ways on a daily basis. The goal is to be both recipients of the seeds of faith and sowers who plant the Word of God as far and wide as possible through our words and deeds.

Soul Gardening: Seeds, Roots, and Branches

To borrow a phrase from my minister-gardener friend, Terry Hershey, this book is about the practice of "soul gardening." Any good gardener is disciplined and knows the practices of stewardship that are most essential to growing a beautiful and fruitful garden. The results speak for themselves. Likewise, any good soul gardener is disciplined about the practices that nurture the seeds of faith so that they grow into a deeply rooted connection with God. The fruits of this garden are freedom, joy, peace, hope, love, and service, which spring forth in the life of a soul gardener.

As spiritual writers such as Richard Foster and Dallas Willard have revealed so well, the Christian tradition is a treasure trove of spiritual disciplines that help us to receive God's gifts of life and grace, and to grow into the people God calls us to be—what Thomas Merton and C.S. Lewis refer to as our "true selves." Without being a how-to manual, this book offers reflections and practices for germinating the seeds of faith in our lives and cultivating a healthy spiritual life. These practices are grounded in Scripture, Christian tradition, and everyday experiences.

Because stories are a powerful vehicle for illustrating a point or moving the spirit, I include stories from my own life and the lives of friends and family whenever they are helpful. While the chapters of this book can be read in any order, they're grouped loosely into three sections that stem from the parable of the sower and build upon each other: Seeds, Roots, and Branches.

The first section, Seeds, may surprise some because in addition to practices such as living fully in the moment, spiritual seeking, solitude, and friendship, it also includes the practice of doubt. Doubt is an essential aspect of faith from Job to Jesus to Augustine to—as many have been surprised to learn—Mother Teresa. Quite simply, doubt is human, and it makes no sense to talk about faith in a way that is disconnected from human experience. This section, then, offers practices to help us mine everyday life for meaning and experiences of God that are the seeds of a deeper faith.

Unlike many spiritual books, this one doesn't presume anything about your faith except that you're interested in exploring it openly and honestly. Early chapters ask you to take stock of where you are on your faith journey, and invite you to walk further down that path.

The second section, Roots, offers practices to help us encourage the seeds of faith, however small they may be, to take root and grow in our lives. These practices include meditation, prayer, worship, spiritual direction, and celebration.

The third section, Branches, offers practices—such as love, vocation, forgiveness, and service—that help us put our faith into action, to be sowers of the Good News. James tells us that "a faith without works is dead," so the healthy faith strives to love, serve, heal, and spread joy. In this section we see more clearly that the heartbeat of Christianity is love and service to others, especially those in the greatest need.

How to Use This Book

It's been said that you haven't read a book once until you've read it twice. Therefore, I encourage you to read this book once straight through (in as few sittings as possible) to get an overall sense of the practices presented here, just as you would scan a garden to appreciate what it has to offer. It will be especially helpful for you to flag the chapters on solitude, meditation, and prayer (chapters 6, 9, and 10, respectively), as they describe the foundational spiritual disciplines you will return to again and again in the life of faith.

On your second read-through, read slowly and intentionally, paying particular attention to each idea as you would the individual flowers in a garden. The very act of reading and reflecting on the content of this book is a spiritual practice that is in tune with other practices such as seeking, study, spiritual exercise, and spiritual reading. Remember, the practice we used for reflecting on and praying with the parable of the sower and the seed can be used with each chapter of this book.

You may wish to read this book on your own, or perhaps with friends and fellow seekers. On your second read-through, read the chapters in any order you prefer, depending on what catches your eye in the garden.

As a final suggestion, you might read and reflect on one chapter per week. You could begin each week by reading and thinking about the recommended practice. Then set aside ten to fifteen minutes each day—perhaps just after waking in the morning, or just before you go to bed—to implement that practice in your life. You could also use the examination of conscience practice described in chapter 14 as a daily exercise, preferably just before you go to bed, to complement your reading of the book.

———————————

Our lives are filled with practices that influence how we eat, sleep, work, raise our kids, spend our free time, and live our lives. It's a simple fact that if we eat well and exercise regularly, we'll be healthier and have more energy for the many people and tasks that demand our attention. The same is true in the spiritual life. If we nourish and exercise our souls through prayer and service, worship and community, we're more inclined to be in tune with God and the joys of life. It is my prayer that the practices in this book help you recognize what God the Gardener is doing in your soul, so that you may have life, and have it abundantly.

ONE SEEDS

Two years ago, I was saying as I planted seeds in the garden, "I must believe in these seeds, that they fall into the earth and grow into flowers and radishes and beans." It is a miracle to me because I do not understand it. The very fact that they use glib technical phrases does not make it any less a miracle, and a miracle we all accept. Then why not accept God's miracles?

—Dorothy Day

Introduction

This first section begins at the beginning, by asking you to reflect on where you are in your faith journey. Each reflection and practice mines life for experiences that might serve as seeds of a faith waiting to take root and push through the surface. The chapters also explore Jesus' life and the Christian tradition for witness and wisdom to help us. Even the most spiritually mature among us benefit from asking anew life's basic questions and reexamining the answers we've come to live by.

Let me begin with a story: While waiting in line to pay for my wife's birthday gift, I spied something called "Lavender in a Bag." Liz loves lavender, so I had to get it. The directions were simple—place the seeds from the seed pouch into the bag containing soil, and add water.

Our son Tyler, then two-and-a-half, was fascinated by this gift. "What is it, a bag of dirt?" he wondered aloud.

We thought about it for a minute. "Well, yes and no."

"What do you mean?" he asked.

"The seeds and dirt in this bag represent how everything in the whole world works."

His big green eyes lit up.

"Just as you need food and love and care, so do these seeds. If we put them in the soil and water them, over time a plant will grow. Eventually the plant will sprout pretty flowers that smell nice."

"I like flowers," he said before peppering us with questions.

When he'd exhausted our knowledge of the natural world,

we explained that each day he could peek inside the bag to see what was happening.

For the first week, Tyler checked the bag every day to find only dirt. He was disappointed, but he held out hope that something would happen.

And something did. When he peeked into the bag on the eighth day, he was thrilled to see small sprouts pushing their way through the soil. Each day thereafter the lavender plants continued to grow, and so did Tyler's enthusiasm.

Driving to work each morning after checking on the lavender plants with my son, I felt an overwhelming sense of peace and clarity. It was good to see my son so excited by nature and to be able to teach him. It was nice to remember my own wonder as a child, experiencing things for the first time. And it was important to be reminded that at its base, life is as simple as seeds, soil, nutrition, sunshine, and growth.

Then, one day, Tyler asked, "Where did the seeds go?"

Jesus' parable of the sower and the seed asks us the same question: where have the seeds of God's Word gone once they've met the soil of our lives? The odds that they're flourishing are not good: They may have fallen on the outskirts of our hearts only to be snatched away by those who think faith is silly. Or perhaps they landed on rocky ground that allowed them to grow for a while, but just wasn't deep enough for roots to take hold. Or perhaps they were choked out by the thorns of our desires for things such as fame or fortune.

But maybe, just maybe, the seeds were able to take root in our souls and are bearing fruit in our lives. The practices in this section are geared toward helping us learn how to recognize the seeds of faith that God sows everywhere and learn how to nurture them to take root in our lives.

For some, talk of God as a sower who spreads seeds of faith is familiar, even exciting. But for many people it's just metaphorical language that has nothing to do with reality. To ground our discussion in the first section of this book, let's be concrete by exploring some of life's big questions: Who are you? Why are you here? What gets you out of bed in the morning? What do you *really* want in life? What do you think about when you're alone? Who are your friends, and what do they mean to you?

All this section, indeed, this book, asks of you is an openness to recognizing these questions and your responses to them as seeds of faith—in God, yourself, and others.

Spiritual wisdom to consider as you identify the seeds of faith in your life:

Though I do not believe that a plant will spring up where no seed has been, I have great faith in a seed. Convince me that you have a seed there, and I am prepared to expect wonders.
—Henry David Thoreau

If seeds in the black earth can turn into such beautiful roses, what might not the heart of man become in its long journey toward the stars?
—G.K. Chesterton

1 Who Am I?
The Practice of *Spirit*-uality

Many spiritual traditions and practices begin with a single question: Who am I? The question is a persistent and intimate companion. The search for our essence, our identity, is fundamental; it is as necessary for individuals as for nations, tribes, races, and spiritual communities. Who am I? Am I spirit or flesh? Am I sacred or secular? Am I irrevocably shaped by the circumstances of my personal history, or am I still free to move and grow, to uncover a new and brighter path? Am I fragile or am I strong, am I broken or am I whole? When I listen deeply to my inner life, what do I hear? What is the substance of my soul, the core of my being? What is my true nature?

—Wayne Muller

REFLECTION

When Rosa Parks refused to give up her bus seat to a white passenger in Montgomery, Alabama, she set in motion a civil rights movement that eventually led to the end of institutionalized segregation in the South. It was 1955, and Montgomery laws required African-Americans to pay their fare to the driver, then get off the bus and reboard through the back door. Sometimes the bus driver would take off before the person could reboard. African-Americans also had to give up their seats to white passengers if the bus was full. On that cold December evening, a forty-two-year-old Rosa Parks refused to give up her seat based solely on the color of her skin. "I did not get on the bus to get arrested," she later said. "I got on the bus to go home."

Imagine if Rosa Parks had been unsure of who she was, if she didn't have a strong sense of herself. She wouldn't have been able to expose the segregation laws for what they were— unjust. And she surely wouldn't have inspired countless others to be courageous enough to stand up for what's right. But Ms. Parks knew who she was, and her legacy lives on.

What adjectives come to mind when you stop and ask yourself, "Who am I?" What feelings surface?

Underneath all the adjectives that we use to describe ourselves and all the feelings that go with those descriptions lies our true nature, the spirit that animates us and makes us who we are. It's easy to get so caught up in life, family, and work that we put our heads down and plough through each day. In some ways, we become actors. But deep inside, we know who we truly are.

Naming our unique spirit is an essential part of living a healthy life and growing as a person.

Naming our spirit tells us what kind of spirituality we practice on a daily basis. Some may object to this notion on the grounds that spirituality belongs to the realm of faith and religion. But spirituality (with a small *s*) is fundamental to being human and is not reliant upon faith or religion. Each one of us has a spirit, an essence, a fire in the belly, a driving force that makes us who we are. The "uality" in the word *spirituality* refers to the way we express the "spirit" that makes us who we are. If our spirit is one of anger, then our lived spirituality—the way we shape and harness our spirit—is to look for reasons to be angry and people at whom to be angry. If our spirit is one of peace, then our lived spirituality is to take things in stride and do our best to maintain balance and perspective. And so on.

In his popular book *The Holy Longing*, Ronald Rolheiser puts it this way:

> Spirituality is not about serenely picking or rationally choosing certain spiritual activities like going to church, praying or meditating, reading spiritual books, or setting off on some explicit spiritual quest. It is far more basic than that. Long before we do anything explicitly religious at all, we have to do something about the fire that burns within us. What we do with that fire, how we channel it, is our spirituality. . . . Spirituality is more about whether or not we can go to sleep at night than about whether or not we go to church. It is about being integrated or falling apart, about being within community or being lonely, about

being in harmony with Mother Earth or being alienated from her.

The human spirit is fueled by fundamental questions common to everyone: Why am I here? Who am I? Where am I going? What do I love? What should I do with my life? How do I become the person I want to be?

Spirituality—tending to our spirit—has to do with asking these questions at various stages in our lives. When we search beyond ourselves to better understand why we are here and what we are to do with our lives, our spirituality takes on a religious dimension and becomes Spirituality with a capital S. Belief and religious practice are ultimately about tapping into the Spirit, the Source of Life, who speaks to our spirits and shapes our understanding of what it means to live with meaning and purpose.

Spirituality with a capital S centers on our human experience of God and finds its expression in religious traditions such as Judaism, Islam, and Christianity. Christian spirituality centers on the lived encounter with Jesus Christ in the Spirit. In this sense, Christian spirituality is concerned not so much with the doctrines of Christianity as with the ways those teachings shape us as individuals and members of society. Through the Incarnation, the central mystery of Christianity, Christ became human like us so that we might become divine like him.

The promise of Christianity is that if we dig beneath our accomplishments and failures, doubts and beliefs, we find that our essential nature is whole and unbroken, as God intended it to be. If we tap into it, we experience a harmony with ourselves and with the world. We gain the courage to be who we really are—made in the image and likeness of God, the Light of the World. And we live our lives more fully in touch with our true purpose.

Thomas Merton said, "There is in all visible things . . . a hidden wholeness." The crucial decision we all must make is whether to live out of this hidden wholeness or to continue living lives that are fragmented and inauthentic.

PRACTICE FOR SPIRITUAL GROWTH

Anais Nin famously said, "We don't see the world *as it is,* we see it as *we are.*"

Who we are shapes how we perceive everything. Our unique spirit expresses itself in a lived spirituality that determines how we see and relate to the people and situations in our lives.

- *Begin your practice by setting aside some quiet time to reread the quotation at the beginning of this chapter and ponder the questions it raises.*
- *Make a list of adjectives and qualities that describe who you are, what you care about, what values you hold most dear. Describe your spirit—what makes you, you?*
- *Reflect on how you see the world and interact with others. If you find it helpful, do this exercise with someone you trust, saying aloud who you are and noticing how you feel as you describe yourself.*

Our spirits are not set in stone. The beauty of being human is that we are free to make choices about who we are and how we want to live. We can change. We can aspire to be our best selves. We can engage in spiritual disciplines that help shape our spirits to be fully alive.

■ *Throughout the course of a day, ask yourself, "Who am I?" When you awake and get ready for your day, ask this question. When you interact with coworkers, eat your meals, read the newspaper, exercise, plop down on the couch, go to bed, ask yourself this question. Who are you when you first awake? Who are you when you interact with family and coworkers? Who are you in each task, each moment? Are you the leader, the follower, the person just trying to skate by? Are you frustrated and angry, or are you happy and at peace?*

■ *Next ask yourself how you feel each time you identify who you are in a given situation. Are you content with your role? Are you embarrassed by your actions? Do you feel authentically yourself in each situation?*

■ *Spend a day noticing the ways in which who you are and how you feel about yourself change. Which descriptions and feelings best represent who you are on the deepest level?*

■ *Next ask yourself, "Who am I when I'm relaxed, on vacation, enjoying a ballgame, reading, exercising, playing with the kids?" How different are you when you're doing something you thoroughly enjoy, as opposed to when you're in the workaday routine? What might you do to bring the aspects of your most free self into the times in your life when you feel most trapped by routine and monotony?*

Finally, reflect on the following quotation from Marianne Williamson's book *A Return to Love:*

Our deepest fear is not that we are inadequate. Our deepest fear is that we are powerful beyond measure. It is our light, not our darkness that most frightens us. We ask ourselves, Who am I to be brilliant, gorgeous, talented, fabulous? Actually, who are you not to be? You are a child of God. Your playing small does not serve the world. There is nothing enlightened about shrinking so that other people won't feel insecure around you. We are all meant to shine, as children do. We were born to make manifest the glory of God that is within us. It's not just in some of us; it's in everyone. And as we let our own light shine, we unconsciously give other people permission to do the same. As we are liberated from our own fear, our presence automatically liberates others.

- *What, if anything, holds you back from being your true, best self?*
- *In the final analysis, what do you want the meaning of your life to have been?*

2 Why Believe?
The Practice of Doubt

Doubt has inspired religion in every age: from Plato, to Augustine, to Descartes, to Pascal, religion has defined itself through doubt's questions. Of course, this extends up to today.

—Jennifer Michael Hecht

Every year I doubt they'll come up. They were a gift—two bags of an assortment of plant bulbs that produce crocuses, tulips, daffodils, and alyssum in stages throughout the spring and early summer. We planted them seven years ago in the impossibly hard, root-laden earth at the base of the trees that line our walkway. We don't take care of them the way real gardeners should. And so each spring I think they can't have the energy to force their way through the ground one more time. And every spring, I am wrong.

I don't want to doubt, but I do. I doubt a lot of things—myself, my career, my loved ones, institutions, God. About the only thing I don't doubt is doubt itself. It dwells in every human heart and takes on many forms, from the seeker to the skeptic, the scientist to the preacher.

Is doubt such a bad thing?

It can be if we let doubt paralyze or diminish us. In its worst forms, doubt fuels fear and cynicism. It convinces us that life is meaningless and that rather than moving closer to our dreams and goals, we are merely marching to our graves. It turns us into cynics—naysayers who scoff at dreams and shoot down enthusiasm. We stand with Shakespeare's Macbeth, who lamented:

Life's but a walking shadow, a poor player,
That struts and frets his hour upon the stage,
and then is heard no more. It is a tale
Told by an idiot, full of sound and fury,
Signifying nothing.

Since the dawning of human consciousness we have looked into the sky and wondered why we are here and what the purpose of our lives is. In our darkest moments, we see ourselves as mere accidents coming from nothing, living for no real reason, and heading back toward nothing. We race to our scientists, philosophers, psychologists, and theologians for explanations and direction. We construct theories and philosophies to comfort and protect us, but we are all swallowed by the shadows at some time or another.

Yet, as paradoxical as it may seem, doubt is a seed of faith. It is essential to the very nature of being human and to belief. Doubt is healthy. It forces us to ask, to think, to seek. It's healthy to doubt our faith and have faith in our doubt.

In the early Middle Ages, religious thinkers began to acknowledge doubt as a central component of belief. Belief is hard, they reasoned, and religion must be a means for us to overcome, even harness, doubts that might otherwise destroy faith.

Since then, Christianity has focused on the stories of doubt that are fundamental to the Hebrew and Christian Scriptures. For example, God promises the aged Abraham and Sarah that they will bear a son, and Sarah doubts. Eventually she does believe, and when her child is born she names him Isaac, which means "may God laugh." Job is tested to the outer reaches of human limits, and he doubts and questions God. Eventually he admits that he cannot possibly understand or judge God's ways, and God restores Job's fortunes twofold. As the Roman authorities seek to apprehend Jesus, his chief disciple, Peter, denies even knowing him. When Jesus is crucified, his disciples lock themselves away in fear, and doubt all that they have seen and been taught. When the resurrected Jesus appears to the dejected disciples on the road to Emmaus, their eyes are blinded by doubt and they do not recognize him.

But it is Jesus' own doubt that is most striking. After celebrating the Passover meal, Jesus asks a few of his disciples to keep watch while he prays in the Garden of Gethsemane. In a profound moment of self-doubt, he turns to Peter and the two sons of Zebedee and tells them, "I am deeply grieved, even to death; remain here, and stay awake with me." The Gospel of Matthew then tells us, "Going a little farther, he threw himself on the ground and prayed, 'My Father, if it is possible, let this cup pass from me; yet not what I want but what you want.'" Jesus asks three times if he really must be crucified, and each time he checks on his companions. Each time, he finds them sleeping. He is alone.

At first, Jesus rebukes them, but eventually he tells them to get their rest. Soon thereafter Judas, whose own doubt leads to the ultimate betrayal, identifies Jesus to the authorities by kissing him on the cheek. Jesus goes calmly with the soldiers, and Judas is so overwhelmed with shame that he takes his own life.

Having carried the instrument of his death to Golgotha, Jesus is nailed to the cross and left to die by crucifixion. This time he doubts God's loyalty when he cries out in agony, "My God, my God, why have you forsaken me?"

On the surface, the Christian story is nothing short of absurd. God sent his only Son to redeem the world. But that Son doubted himself and his purpose, was rejected by the very people he came to save, and eventually died an excruciating death on a cross as a blasphemer.

And yet, it is Jesus the doubter who, as the Christ of faith, understands our own doubt better than we do ourselves. Take, for example, the story of Thomas. When the resurrected Jesus first appeared to the disciples, Thomas was not with them.

Upon hearing his friends' story of having seen Jesus, he was incredulous: "Unless I see the mark of the nails in his hands, and put my finger in the mark of the nails and my hand in his side, I will not believe."

A week after the resurrected Jesus appeared to them, the disciples, including Thomas, were all together in a locked house when Jesus "came and stood among them and said, 'Peace be with you.' Then he said to Thomas, 'Put your finger here and see my hands. Reach out your hand and put it in my side. Do not doubt but believe.'"

The good news is that while Jesus praises those who believe in him without having seen, he invites the greatest of doubters to seek the evidence we need so that our doubt does not slip into disbelief.

PRACTICE FOR SPIRITUAL GROWTH

As a discipline, naming and facing our doubts from time to time is a key step toward spiritual growth. We all doubt at times in our lives. What we do with and because of our doubt is what really matters.

- *Imagine yourself in the scene as the disciples tell Thomas of their encounter with the risen Christ. If you put yourself in Thomas's shoes, how would you react? Would you believe your friends' story, or would you still need to see and touch the risen Christ for yourself? Even if you believed your friends, would you still touch Jesus' side?*

- *Alone or with a partner, reflect on what you most doubt and why. Do you doubt yourself? Do you doubt that your life has meaning and purpose? Do you doubt the intentions and integrity of others? Do you doubt institutional religion? God's existence? Or that we are made to be happy?*

- *Now, reflect on how your doubts affect the way you live your life. Do they cause you to live timidly? Do they drive you to cynicism? Do your doubts prompt you to probe more deeply into the reasons for and meaning behind the events of life? Do they help you live more intentionally and richly? Do they help you enjoy your convictions more because they don't come easily?*

- *When you have finished exploring basic doubts and how they may affect the way you live, ask yourself which of your doubts are the strongest. Are there any that you wish to overcome? What might you do to rid yourself of any doubts that get in the way of living a healthy, happy life?*

- *How does Jesus' compassion for and willingness to help those who doubt speak to your life today? In what ways can your faith help you face your doubts and free you to be your best self?*

3 Awareness
The Practice of Seeking

Most people, even thought they don't know it, are asleep. They're born asleep, they live asleep, they marry asleep, they breed children in their sleep, they die in their sleep without ever waking up. They never understand the loveliness and the beauty of this thing that we call human existence.
                    —Anthony de Mello, SJ

REFLECTION

Awareness is both a blessing and a curse. One the one hand, we humans are able to appreciate life more fully than any other creature. We savor nice weather, conversations with friends, good meals, moments of peaceful solitude, helping others, being loved. We seek meaning and try to make the most out of life.

On the other hand, we are always aware that life is short and filled with struggles and suffering. For some, this awareness leads to despair and a desire to numb the senses. As de Mello's quote above suggests, most people don't recognize that the disciplines they practice on a daily basis deaden their senses and keep them focused on the mundane rather than the extraordinary. Nothing could be more harmful to the faith life.

To help us realize why awareness is such a powerful seed of faith, the great Christian thinker C.S. Lewis wrote *The Screwtape Letters*. In the story, Screwtape is a senior devil from a highly organized and technologically savvy hell who writes letters instructing his junior demon nephew, Wormwood, how to patiently win over a young man's soul. The first and most important of Screwtape's letters instructs Wormwood to keep his "patient's" focus on daily life and nothing more.

Distractions are easy, Screwtape says, because humans "find it all but impossible to believe in the unfamiliar while the familiar is before their eyes." He cautions, however, that trying to plant ideas and arguments in his patient's head is a bad idea:

By the very act of arguing, you awake the patient's reason; and once it is awake, who can forsee the result? Even if a particular train of thought can be twisted so as to end in our favor, you will find that you have been strengthening in your patient the fatal habit of attending to universal issues and withdrawing his attention from the stream of immediate sense experiences. Your business is to fix his attention on the stream. Teach him to call it "real life" and don't let him ask what he means by "real."

Don't you sometimes feel like you're losing a battle with forces that conspire to keep your focus away from what really matters in life? I, for one, buy into the promise that technology and various gadgets will make my life more organized and efficient, but in the end I still don't have time for quiet reflection. When I'm not checking off to-do list items on my "personal digital assistant," I'm writing and reading e-mail, taking detours on the Web as flashing buttons tempt me to "click here," talking on my cell phone, listening to my MP3 player, attending meetings. All the while I am bombarded with ads for more gadgets and products I (probably) don't need. My most recent stab at resisting the pervasive consumer culture was to hook up a digital video recorder to my television so I can fast-forward through commercials. But advertisers are already a step ahead with product placements on the sets of popular shows and signs against the backstops of our favorite ballparks. They've even printed their ads on the shells of the eggs we buy at the supermarket for our hurried morning breakfasts!

All of the noise and chaos of my daily life drowns out the whispers of my soul as it seeks meaning. It even drowns out spirit, doubt, and wonder.

Screwtape smiles. His work is easy.

And yet. And yet, grace enters my life and makes sure I am awake. A loved one dies or faces a serious illness. My children laugh so hard they can barely breathe. My wife and I support each other through tough times and enjoy quiet evenings and long walks together. I am surprised by someone else's care. And I wonder: Are we really all alone in this universe, or is there a God? Can we tap into ultimate reality and find true meaning?

Screwtape worries: "The characteristic of Pains and Pleasures is that they are unmistakably real, and therefore, as far as they go, give the [person] who feels them a touchstone of reality."

A recent drive home from the office provided me with just such a touchstone of reality. After a particularly busy day, my head was filled with the noise of meetings, phone calls, and thoughts about how to meet goals at work *and* be a good husband and dad. As the news radio bounced from shootings to sports, and billboards encouraged me to treat myself to a massage or buy a new car, I wanted to hit pause.

Just then, I looked up to see if the traffic light was green and caught the sun breaking through the clouds one last time before going down for the night. My senses were awakened and for a moment I was aware of God's presence. But before I could ponder more deeply, I was home.

Screwtape sighs in relief. If a patient comes into contact with a touchstone of reality, he advises Wormwood, "the great thing is to prevent his doing anything . . . to sterilize the seeds which the Enemy plants in a human soul. . . . The more he feels without acting, the less he will be able ever to act, and in the long run the less he will be able to feel."

But it's too late, the seed has stirred, and T.S. Eliot's wisdom comes to mind:

We had the experience but missed the meaning
And approach to the meaning restores the experience
In a different form, beyond any meaning
We can assign to happiness.

Later that night, after reading stories to the kids and tucking them into bed, I sat motionless in the dark bedroom, listening to their breathing and going over my day. I thought more about the sunset and the things that really matter, and for the time being, Screwtape was at bay.

PRACTICE FOR SPIRITUAL GROWTH

"The unexamined life is not worth living," Socrates tells us. And yet, it's easy to float (or ride the rapids) from one day to the next without being awake, aware, alive.

If Christianity's about anything, it's about living an examined life and seeking meaning. Jesus himself remains one of the most passionate seekers of all time. He sought to understand his purpose on earth, and once he found it, he devoted his life to spreading justice, love, mercy, healing, and reconciliation.

Jesus' great question to us all is, "What do you seek?" In the Gospel of John, for example, John the Baptist is standing with two of his disciples when he sees Jesus walk by; John exclaims, "Look, here is the Lamb of God!" With great shock and fascination, John's followers leave their leader's side and begin to follow Jesus. They want to see for themselves why John so reveres this man. As Jesus continues on his way, he is keenly aware that he is being followed. Eventually, he turns to the curious disciples and asks, "What do you seek?"

Nearly two thousand years later, Jesus continues to ask his followers, "What do you seek?" He invites all of us to bring our questioning, doubting selves to him. He tells us time and again: "Ask, and it will be given you; search, and you will find; knock, and the door will be opened for you. For everyone who asks receives, and everyone who searches finds, and for everyone who knocks, the door will be opened."

PRACTICE FOR SPIRITUAL GROWTH

■ *Take a moment to reflect on your life at this moment. Following the pattern of reflection outlined in the introduction to this book, reflect on the quotation from Anthony de Mello at the beginning of this chapter. If you wish, record your thoughts in a journal.*

■ *Consider your daily life: Are you asleep or awake? Are you just going through the motions in your life, or are you an active participant? What would Wormwood make of you? Would you be an easy or difficult "patient" for him to distract from deeper thoughts of God, meaning, life? Why or why not?*

■ *Now, reflect on what you most seek in life right now: What role, if any, does faith play in your quest for a full life? Do you believe God plants desires in your heart? That God guides you in your journey to find what you are looking for? Why or why not?*

■ *Finally, begin each week by naming what you seek most in life at the moment and developing a plan to pursue your goals. Tell your spouse or a trusted friend about your plan and ask him or her to help keep you on track in achieving it.*

4 What Do I *Really* Want?
The Practice of Feeding Our Deepest Human Hungers

It is quite true that man lives by bread alone—when there is no bread. But what happens to man's desires when there is plenty of bread and when his belly is chronically filled? At once other (and "higher") needs emerge and these, rather than physiological hungers, dominate the organism. And when these in turn are satisfied, again new (and still "higher") needs emerge and so on. . . .

The human being is simultaneously that which he is and that which he yearns to be.

—Abraham Maslow

REFLECTION

What are your deepest hungers? Beneath your immediate goals and obligations, what do you *really* hunger for?

These seemingly simple questions grow more complex as we move through life. As children, we were filled with untamed wonder and awe; we knew our hungers and we pursued them with everything we had. Remember running freely through fields with your friends? Remember pulling aside the tepee-shaped branches of an evergreen and pretending you'd stepped into another world? Remember lying on your back and staring deeply into the night sky, diving into a pile of leaves, telling stories and laughing so hard your belly hurt, racing down a snowy hill on your fastest sled, dreaming you could fly? Fueled by the sense of trust and freedom that are the rights of childhood, we naturally pursued our passions and fed our hunger to know, to live, to love. The universe was our playground and in it we laughed and asked questions like "How?" and, more important, "Why?"

It's not that we lose our imaginations or intimacy with the universe as we grow older; it's that we learn to keep our heads down. We're more cautious after experiencing loss and loneliness, betrayal and disappointment at different stages in our lives. We're busy, and, truth be told, we like it that way. And we're constantly distracted and tempted by what the world tells us we need to be, do, and buy to be successful and happy.

Yet, in the midst of it all, we are occasionally awakened to our deepest hungers and reminded that there is something more at work in the world. A loved one falls ill, and in caring for her we realize how precious life is. A child's smile fills us with love; a sunset draws us to a larger horizon of hope; a simple question from a friend—"How are you?"—tears down the fortresses we build around our hearts.

While these moments of clarity about what really matters are fleeting, they connect us to the deeper reality of who we are and what we desire. They make us stop and listen to our hungers for love, companionship, freedom, peace, truth, goodness, meaning, and happiness.

Driven by a desire to come face to face with his deepest hungers, Henry David Thoreau famously traded the comforts of his home in Concord, Massachusetts, for a ten-by-fifteen-foot log cabin he built on the shore of nearby Walden Pond. "I went to the woods," he later wrote in *Walden,* "because I wished to live deliberately, to front only the essential facts of life, and see if I could not learn what it had to teach and not, when I came to die, discover that I had not lived. . . . I wanted to live deep and suck the marrow out of life." For two years, two months, and two days (from July 4, 1845, through September 6, 1847), Thoreau lived simply and chronicled the reflection of his soul in the pond and the natural world around him. He came away with many insights that flow from one simple truth, "To be awake is to be alive":

We must learn to reawaken and keep ourselves awake, not by mechanical aids, but by an infinite expectation of the dawn, which does not forsake us in our soundest sleep. . . . When we are unhurried and wise, we perceive that only great and worthy things have any permanent and absolute existence—that petty fears and petty pleasures are but the shadow of the reality.

When we deny our deepest hungers, warns Thoreau, we run the risk of living in the shadows of reality and being untrue to ourselves. What begins as a shadow can quickly become an all-encompassing darkness that blinds us to who we really are. But when we name our hungers, such as wanting to be accepted and loved, we move out of the shadows.

This talk of shadows and light would have sounded foreign to us when we were kids. "Children, who play life," says Thoreau, "discern its true law and relations more clearly than men, who fail to live it worthily." By "playing life" we lived genuinely. We were ourselves, and we were more comfortable believing that we came from a loving Creator who took joy in our discoveries. So, what prevents us from "playing life" today?

At the center of every human heart is a hunger for something more. Even the greatest skeptic or most committed atheist can't help asking what life is all about and if there is more to the story than meets the eye.

Religious traditions are rooted in the understanding that there is, indeed, more to life than meets the eye. The Judeo-Christian tradition names the "more" God and invites us to see how our deepest hungers come from and are fed by God. As the story in John's Gospel of Jesus and the woman at the well illustrates, Jesus spent his entire life and ministry trying to open our eyes to the reality of God. In the story, a tired Jesus stops at Jacob's well in Samaria on his way from Judea to Galilee. There he encounters a Samaritan woman and asks her for a drink. She is surprised at the request because Jews and Samaritans were typically hostile to each other, and the following exchange ensues:

> Jesus answered her, "If you knew the gift of God, and who it is that is saying to you, 'Give me a drink,' you would have asked him, and he would have given you living water." The woman said to him, "Sir, you have no bucket, and the well is deep. Where do you get that living water? Are you greater than our ancestor Jacob, who gave us the well, and with his sons and his flocks drank from it?" Jesus said to her, "Everyone who drinks of this water will be thirsty again, but those who drink of the water that I will give them will never be thirsty. The water that I will give will become in them a spring of water gushing up to eternal life."

Once the woman recognized Jesus as the Messiah, she "left her water jar" and returned to the city to tell others of her encounter. Just then, the disciples urge Jesus to eat something. He responds, "I have food to eat that you do not know about. . . . My food is to do the will of him who sent me and to complete his work."

Though the disciples had the advantage of witnessing firsthand Jesus' ministry and miracles, they repeatedly fail to understand the message he gives over and over again: "I am the bread of life. Whoever comes to me will never be hungry, and whoever believes in me will never be thirsty." All these years later, it's even more difficult for us to understand how Jesus can satisfy our deepest human hungers.

The quotation by Abraham Maslow that began this chapter provides a path to understanding. Whether we call ourselves religious or not, to reach the highest heights of human fulfillment, we must be free to focus beyond our physiological need for bread. In too many parts of the world, starvation continues to claim people's lives and spirits, and we have a moral obligation to do what we can to alleviate it. For those of us fortunate enough to have our basic needs for food, clothing, and shelter met, a problem arises when we remain focused on the "bread" before our eyes—our job, bank account, reputation, possessions, and the like. According to Maslow, to be our best selves, we must move beyond material needs to feed our needs for love, intimacy, belonging, self-esteem, self-worth, creativity, and meaning.

When Jesus says, "One does not live by bread alone, but by every word that comes from the mouth of God," he is calling us to name our deepest hungers and connect with God as the greatest source of nourishment for our lives. The promise is that our hungers will be fed: "Blessed are you who hunger now, for you will be filled."

PRACTICE FOR SPIRITUAL GROWTH

This week set aside an hour in which you can be still and think about your life and your deepest hungers. You might take a walk in the woods or sit in your favorite quiet spot at home. The point is to find a time and a place where you are free from all distractions. If you find it helpful, write down the images, words, and emotions that come to mind as you reflect.

■ *Begin by thinking about your childhood: What did you love to do? What made you laugh? What are your fondest memories? What lessons did you learn from your family? Who were your friends? What did you love most about them? What did they love most about you? What were you really good at? What did you do when nobody else was looking, just because you enjoyed it? What were your dreams? What did you want to be when you grew up?*

■ *Now, think about your life today: Who are you? What do you love? Who are your friends, and what do you love about each other? Do you love what you do for a living? Why or why not? What losses, disappointments, and defeats have shaped you? What frustrates you most? What makes you happiest? What do you enjoy most in life? What do you want most in life right now?*

■ *As you look at who you were as a child and who you are now, what strikes you most? Are you living the life you once dreamed of? Are you happy? Do you find meaning in life? Do you believe your life matters? Do you know where you are going in life?*

■ *Now reflect on your deepest hungers at this point in your life. If it's helpful, write them down before you begin. Do any of your hungers surprise you? Are there any hungers that God may have planted in you to help you awaken and focus your energy in a more life-giving direction? Do you believe that God seeks us as we seek God? Is it possible that God is trying to get your attention?*

- *Think about the ways your hungers are satisfied: Do you talk about them with friends and family? Do you write about them or pray about them? Does attending church help you?*

- *Consider what keeps you from satisfying your hungers: Are you too busy? Do you fear who you really are? Are you caught up in a life you seem to have no control over?*

- *Consider the changes you can make to live more authentically according to your deepest hungers: Aside from moving to a cabin in the woods as Thoreau did, identify one thing you could do to live more intentionally and deeply and commit to doing it as a daily discipline. Keep a journal or share with a friend your experiences living more intentionally.*

5 Living Fully in the Moment
The Practice of Presence

*Mindfulness frees us of forgetfulness and dispersion and
makes it possible to live fully each minute of life. Mindfulness
enables us to live.*

—Thich Nhat Hanh

REFLECTION

Perhaps you've experienced a life-changing event that
taught you how precious every moment of life is. For me,
such an event happened when I was in my mid-twenties. One
night I was jolted from my sleep because my heart was racing
out of control. No matter what I did, I couldn't get it to slow
down. I'd never felt more exhausted in my life, yet I couldn't
rest. I phoned my mother; "Relax and breathe deeply," she said,
with great concern in her voice. We stayed on the phone into

the early hours of the morning, talking to get my mind off of what was happening.

I got myself to a physician as soon as his office opened the next morning. "You've had an episode of tachycardia, or extreme acceleration of the heart rate," he said. The specialist determined that I have an irregular heartbeat that can be exacerbated by stress. "Your options," he said, "are to go on beta-blockers to regulate your heartbeat, which can make you feel tired and depressed, or you can live with a sensitivity to the irregularities." I chose to live with the irregularities. "You should do everything you can," the doctor added, "to avoid stress."

At twenty-five I was forced to stop and listen to my heart. It had physically awakened me from a deep sleep, and now it was trying to awaken me from a different kind of sleep—a lack of awareness about the stressful life I was living. Whenever any of us comes to the realization that the life we're living might be killing us, it's natural to search for solutions.

As it turned out, I found my solution in a used bookstore when I came across a tattered copy of *The Miracle of Mindfulness,* by Thich Nhat Hanh. For $2.50, I learned one of the most valuable lessons of my life: "While washing the dishes one should only be washing the dishes."

Up until that point in my life, I'd washed the dishes as I did so many other things: as quickly as I could to get to other, seemingly more important things. Why put any more emphasis on washing the dishes than necessary? Because, explains Nhat Hanh, "that's precisely the point. The fact that I am standing there and washing these bowls is a wondrous reality. I'm being completely myself, following my breath, conscious of my presence, and conscious of my thoughts and actions. There's no way I can be tossed around mindlessly like a bottle slapped here and there on the waves."

Mindfulness means keeping our consciousness alive to the present reality. It means being aware of the miracle of life. "People usually consider walking on water or in thin air a miracle," says Nhat Hanh. "But I think the real miracle is not to walk either on water or in thin air, but to walk on earth. Every day we are engaged in a miracle which we don't even recognize: a blue sky, white clouds, green leaves, the curious eyes of a child—our own two eyes. All is a miracle."

Mindfulness, then, is both a seed and a fruit.

A little-known eighteenth-century French Jesuit named Jean-Pierre de Caussade wrote a book called *Abandonment to Divine Providence,* in which he develops the concept of "the sacrament of the present moment." Every moment, he says, is given to us by God and thus bears God's will for us. For Caussade, living in a spirit of mindfulness and abandonment allows our lives to become texts: "The Holy Spirit writes no more Gospels except in our hearts. All we do from moment to moment is live this new gospel of the Holy Spirit. We, if we are holy, are the paper; our sufferings and our actions are the ink. The workings of the Holy Spirit are his pen, and with it he writes a living gospel."

By practicing the sacrament of the present moment, we allow the Holy Spirit to write on the paper of our lives. The question we should ask ourselves is, "In the final analysis, what will the text of our lives convey?"

Treating each moment as a sacrament teaches us how to focus, concentrate, and be present to the miracle of life. Over time, this practice becomes a way of life—a life of awareness that enables us to live fully in each moment.

This all sounds wonderful, but the reality is that we are busy and have grown so accustomed to being pulled in a million directions that we can barely hear the still small voice that cries out for peace and integration. Henri Nouwen illustrates this point well in a meditation he wrote when he returned to America for a visit from the l'Arche Daybreak community in Toronto, Canada, where he shared the final years of his life with a group of people with disabilities:

> What most strikes me, being back in the United States, is the full force of the restlessness, the loneliness, and the tension that holds so many people. The conversations I had today were about spiritual survival. So many of my friends feel overwhelmed by the many demands made on them; few feel the inner peace and joy they so much desire. . . . There seems to be a mountain of obstacles preventing people from being where their hearts want to be. It is so painful to watch and experience. The astonishing thing is that the battle for survival has become so "normal" that few people really believe that it can be different.

But it can be different. The first step of practicing the sacrament of the present moment is to awaken to the common problem John Lennon summarized when he said, "Life is what happens to you when you are busy making other plans." In other words, we often spend so much time planning a life of meaning and happiness that we forget to live the life we have. The side effects of this way of life are stress from worrying if our plans will work out, and disappointment and sorrow when they don't. We often then let our past failures hold us back from living more freely and fully.

The second step is to stop and listen to the questions of our hearts, including the ones we typically avoid: Am I too busy? Have I neglected friends and family? Am I happy? Do my goals and ambitions match up with who I am and what I believe is most meaningful in life? If not, what can I do to live more fully?

The third step is learn how to master and restore our dispersed minds to wholeness so that we can truly live each moment of life. Like many, my greatest challenge is to live an integrated life in which I don't divide myself and my time into parts—one for my wife, another for my kids, another for my job, and so on. There's only one outcome to this way of life: frustration at how little of "my time" is actually left over for me. By practicing mindfulness, every moment becomes "my time," whether I'm completing a task at work, spending time with family and friends, or even washing the dishes. By living this way, I savor the time I am able to spend reading, writing, exercising, and relaxing without coveting them as different from or more enjoyable than the time I spend being present to my family, friends, and coworkers.

The miracle of mindfulness is that we can be fully alive right here, right now, even in the most mundane moments. By paying attention to simple acts such as washing the dishes, getting dressed in the morning, commuting to work, we become more integrated and peaceful and, therefore, better equipped to handle trials and savor joys. We also become more capable of recognizing and nurturing the seeds of faith that God plants in our lives.

Today, when I am aware of my heartbeat, irregularities and all, I consider life a miracle. My prayer is that with each beat I am better able to know God and live fully in each moment of my life.

PRACTICE FOR SPIRITUAL GROWTH

Hanging in my aunt's kitchen is a handmade banner that reads: "This is the day the Lord has made, let us rejoice and be glad in it." Growing up, I wondered what that meant. Be glad for what? Rejoice how? Then one day it hit me: Be glad to be alive, and rejoice by making the most of each day. "That's right," my aunt said. "Every day is sacred."

- ■ *Find a quiet place where you can be still and meditate. Sit in a comfortable position and close your eyes.*
- ■ *Now, breathe in slowly until your lungs are filled with air. As you breathe in, be aware of how the air feels as it passes through your nose and into your lungs. Hold your breath for a few seconds, and then breathe out until your lungs are empty. As you exhale, be mindful of how it feels to release the air from your lungs. Repeat this process for five minutes, slowly inhaling and exhaling as you clear your mind of everything except the awareness of your lungs filling and emptying.*

▪ *As your mind clears, spend another five minutes focusing on simply being in the moment. Resist the temptation to think about your day, job, duties at home, or to-do list. Just be. Breathe in, breathe out. In, and out. Be mindful of your heartbeat and the rest of your body. Allow yourself to marvel at how complex and amazing your body is. Feel the life that courses through your veins.*

▪ *At the end of your session, slowly open your eyes and readjust to your environment. Write down any thoughts, images, and feelings you experienced as you were being mindful of your breathing and body. Reflect on how this moment is a sacrament that conveys God's gifts of life and awareness.*

▪ *Finally, reflect on how you might apply this experience of mindfulness in your daily life. Many people wait to relax and "be themselves" until they take a vacation or go on a retreat. But mindfulness is something you can practice even in the midst of your most hectic days. Repeating this exercise will help you train yourself to be mindful of the present moment and the gifts of your life, so that you can live fully in each moment of each day.*

It is very helpful to set aside at least one day each week in which you can be completely mindful from the time you awake until you fall asleep. As you wake, be mindful of your breathing and get out of bed slowly. Greet the day with a smile, and marvel at what it means to be alive. When you shower, be mindful of the the sensation of the water hitting your skin, the smell of the soap and shampoo, the act of washing your hair and body. When you brush your teeth, brush your teeth. When you dress, think about each step in the process. As you complete these acts, focus on your breathing. Carry this practice through every moment of your day, from eating your breakfast to doing chores, reading, and relaxing. Don't do anything for the sake of just getting it done; rather, be completely mindful of each task and take things slowly.

■ *At the end of your day, consider the miracle of your life and give thanks. If you so desire, read Scripture or something of a spiritual nature to sharpen your focus on the sacredness of life. Before you go to sleep, review your day: Was being intentional and mindful rewarding? What seeds of faith did God plant in your life today? What will you do to help them take root and grow? What are you most grateful for at this moment? How will you carry this gratitude into tomorrow? The rest of the week?*

■ *Prepare yourself to be more mindful tomorrow, no matter what the day has in store for you.*

6 Loneliness vs. Being Alone
The Practice of Solitude

But now more than ever the word about Jesus spread abroad; many crowds would gather to hear him and to be cured of their diseases. But he would withdraw to deserted places and pray.

—Luke 5:15–16

REFLECTION

A close friend of mine suffers from seasonal affective disorder (SAD), a form of depression that commonly hits people in the winter. Each year, as the season's canopy of gray clouds covers his part of the country, my friend changes. Despite having a very successful career, he loses confidence in his abilities. Though he's a physically fit athlete, he becomes lethargic. In spite of being happily married and having a loving family, he feels lonely. It's the loneliness, he says, that causes him to suffer most. Before he sought help and was treated for SAD, my friend said, "Nights were the worst because I'd lie next to my wife and feel lonely, which then made me feel guilty and ashamed."

Whether or not we suffer from depression, we all feel lonely at times. Loneliness can emerge through a lack of meaningful friendships, alienation by a person or group, the breakup of a marriage or relationship, the loss of a loved one, moving from a familiar job or place. We can also feel lonely after positive events such as a wedding, the birth of a child, or a major accomplishment in school or our career. Loneliness is more than simply desiring companionship; it's the experience of feeling profound emptiness even in the midst of loved ones.

Loneliness, paradoxically, occurs most often in heavily populated cities. Today, one in five Americans reports feeling lonely much of the time. In addition to causing feelings of unhappiness, loneliness leads to high blood pressure and such issues as impaired sleep, a weakened immune system, alcoholism, and suicide.

Naturally, we fear loneliness because of how it makes us feel physically, emotionally, and spiritually. Consciously or unconsciously, we try to combat it by keeping busy and filling the quiet with noise. We seek anything that will stifle the voice in us that says we're insignificant and life is meaningless. In the end, all we accomplish is staging a no-win battle between loneliness and distraction.

There is, however, another way to get through life: learning how to be alone. Psychologists make good livings teaching us that if we can learn to be truly intimate with ourselves, then we are never really alone. By facing the complete picture of who we are, wounds and all, and learning to love ourselves, we cease to rely on others for our self-worth or to seek distractions to stave off feelings of loneliness. As a result, we are better able to enter into relationships and enjoy life, even when we are alone.

The Christian tradition takes a different approach. Rather than simply teach us how to be alone with ourselves, Christianity teaches us to embrace solitude as a means to connecting with God and, ultimately, our purpose. In solitude, we discover that we are never alone because God is always with us.

Throughout his life, Jesus experienced profound loneliness. As Mother Teresa explains:

> When Christ said: "I was hungry and you fed me," he didn't mean only the hunger for bread and for food; he also meant the hunger to be loved. Jesus himself experienced this loneliness. He came amongst his own and his own received him not, and it hurt him then and it has kept on hurting him. The same hunger, the same loneliness, the same having no one to be accepted by and to be loved and wanted by. Every human being in that case resembles Christ in his loneliness; and that is the hardest part, that's real hunger.

The good news is that if we resemble Christ in his hunger for love and pain in loneliness, we also resemble him in his ability to embrace solitude as a necessary path to connecting with God and understanding our purpose on earth.

Matthew's Gospel tells us that before he began his public ministry, Jesus spent forty days in the desert, alone. Many times throughout his ministry, he "spent the night alone," "withdrew to a lonely place," "went up to the hills by himself," and "withdrew to the wilderness to pray." As a youth, he spent hours in silence and solitude studying the Torah and trying to understand who he was and what he was supposed to do with his life. We can imagine him learning the craft of carpentry from his earthly father, Joseph, and pondering his life in solitude as he transformed trees into doors, tables, and chairs. Or walking great distances to attend synagogue or retrieve water and food for his household.

On the night before he was betrayed by Judas and taken into custody, Jesus went with three of his disciples to the Garden of Gethsemane to pray in solitude. He instructed his companions, "Sit here while I go over there and pray." Then he said to them, "I am deeply grieved, even to death; remain here, and stay awake with me." After going a little farther away from his friends, he threw himself to the ground and prayed, "My Father, if it is possible, let this cup pass from me."

In his solitude, he was able to be most genuinely himself—a human being afraid of death. He was able to pray, to plead with God to let him live. But, more important, in his solitude Jesus was able to trust God to the point that he could pray in the very next breath, "Yet not what I want but what you want."

Three times he returned to his disciples and found them sleeping instead of keeping watch, and three times, he went away alone and prayed, "My Father, if this cannot pass unless I drink it, your will be done."

After the third period of intense prayer, Jesus returned to his friends and said, "Get up, let us be going." In his solitude, Jesus accepted his mission to teach the good news that we are never alone, that love is the meaning of life, and that death is not the end.

In his book *Celebration of Discipline,* Richard Foster explains, "Loneliness is inner emptiness. Solitude is inner fulfillment." In solitude, as Henri Nouwen observed, we hear the voice of the one who says, "You are my beloved." For Jesus, listening to this voice allowed him to be who he was meant to be, even when he was rejected and scorned and crucified. Knowing he was God's beloved allowed him to move out from his interior self to be in community with his disciples and those on the margins, and to minister to those in need. By learning to practice solitude, we grow in our own faith and learn to do the same.

PRACTICE FOR SPIRITUAL GROWTH

Solitude is the foundation for meditation, prayer, and many other disciplines that lead to a healthy faith life. Learn to practice solitude, and you'll find yourself better in tune with God, yourself, and others.

■ *A first step in practicing solitude is learning to take advantage of "mini retreats" or "little solitudes" that comprise our days. Ideally, these moments of solitude will also be silent, such as when you first wake up or while you sip your coffee before work. More likely, they'll include the noise of everyday life as you make your way through traffic or ride in an elevator or wait on hold for someone on the other end of the phone.*

The point is to make the most out of these moments by quieting the noise within yourself and being present to the here and now rather than becoming impatient or getting lost in to-do lists and worries.

■ *Additional steps in practicing solitude include setting aside a small block of time each day to rest and recharge, limiting how much you speak (try to go an entire day without speaking!), and designating a quiet place (inside or outside your home) and a time when you can retreat there for a regular period of solitude and silence. One of the hardest things about the practice of solitude is to do nothing except be still and listen. Practice is the key.*

■ *To take your practice of solitude further, try to get away for a few half- or full-day periods each year. Or, if possible, go on a retreat for two days or more. Take little more with you than a change of clothes, a Bible, and a journal. Use this time to reevaluate where you are in life: Where do you want to be in three years? In five years? In seven years?*

7 Companions on the Journey
The Practice of Friendship

Faithful friends are a sturdy shelter:
whoever finds one has found a treasure.
Faithful friends are beyond price;
no amount can balance their worth.
Faithful friends are life-saving medicine;
and those who fear the Lord will find them.
—Sirach 6:14–16

REFLECTION

If you know who Mister Rogers is, you probably consider him a friend. Through his television show, *Mister Rogers' Neighborhood,* he reached out to us personally, and told us we are special and we matter, just as we are. He taught us not to pretend to be anybody else or to hide our feelings. Then he took us all around his fascinating neighborhood and introduced us to his friends and showed us what it meant to help them, listen to them, and enjoy their company. He never talked down to anyone, he was never in a hurry, and everything he said made sense.

It wasn't until I was much older that I learned Fred Rogers was an ordained Presbyterian minister who believed deeply in God's love and friendship. Looking back now, I see that everything about his show—from the adventures he took us on to the original songs he sang—invited us to experience God's love so that, in turn, we could love ourselves and other people. Around the time of his death in 2003, "friends of Fred" everywhere swapped their favorite Mister Rogers quotes. Since then I've saved two nuggets of wisdom that are worth quoting here:

> If we're really honest with ourselves, there are probably times when we think, "What possible use can I be in this world? What need is there for somebody like me to fill?" That's one of the deeper mysteries. Then God's grace comes to us in the form of another person who tells us we have been of help, and what a blessing that is.

> I remember one of my seminary professors saying people who were able to appreciate others—who looked for what was good and healthy and kind—were about as close as you could get to God—to the eternal good. And those people who were always looking for what was *bad* about themselves and others were really on the side of evil. "That's what evil wants," he would say. "Evil wants us to feel so terrible about who we are and who we know, that we'll

look with condemning eyes on anybody who happens to be with us at the moment." I encourage you to look for the good where you are and embrace it.

Something of a Mister Rogers of the twelfth century, Aelred of Rievaulx wrote an innovative and timeless book entitled *Spiritual Friendship* that makes the bold claim that not only can we become friends of God, we are *called* to be friends of God because "God *is* friendship."

Aelred was born in Northumbria (between England and Scotland) and raised at the Royal Court of Scotland. While in the service of King David of Scotland in 1134, he visited the Cistercian monastery of Rievaulx in Yorkshire and was so taken by his encounter with the monks that he joined them the next day. Until that time, he felt spiritually empty and was turned off by the culture of greed and shallow friendships he had experienced. Thirteen years later, he became abbot of Rievaulx, and for the rest of his life recorded his reflections and conversations about friendship to help his monks avoid false friendships rooted in human sinfulness (such as hunger for power, jealousy, manipulation, and self-centeredness) in favor of spiritual, or true, friendships rooted in God, charity, and good will. For Aelred, all love, all friendship, has its source in God; therefore, to befriend our neighbor is to befriend God, and to befriend God is to befriend our neighbor.

For Aelred, "spiritual friendship" is friendship *with* God, *of* God, and *for* God. What this means becomes most clear in Jesus Christ, who teaches us to love God intimately as Abba, or "Papa"; who gathers us in community with others of faith, as the Gospel of Matthew conveys, by stating, "For where two or three are gathered in my name, I am there among you"; and who calls us to love everyone, most especially those on the margins, as God loves us.

This last point is the defining characteristic of Christian friendship. Whereas traditional friendship (*philia*) is preferential (to have a friend is to prefer one type of person over another), Christian friendship (*agape*) is universal, unconditional, and open to all. Likewise, while the golden rule—"Love your neighbor as yourself"—is a good formula for living a moral life, Christ goes further by challenging us to "love one another *as I have loved you.*"

Loving as Jesus loved is not an abstract concept; it's an essential practice in the Christian life. Loving as Jesus loved means loving others for who they are and helping them be their best selves. It means going out of our way to love those who are marginalized, rejected, discriminated against, teased, diminished. It means befriending God so that we can love the people God loves.

As in Mister Rogers' neighborhood, God's neighborhood is all-inclusive and values each person as special and worthy of love. If we come to see ourselves as members of God's neighborhood, we seek friendships rooted in God and focused on making the neighborhood a safe, joyful, and loving place for everyone. In the words of his good friend Fred Rogers, God asks each of us, "Won't you be my neighbor?"

PRACTICE FOR SPIRITUAL GROWTH

The word *friend* is used to describe a wide range of relationships. A recent study shows that common types of friendships fall under two categories: simple friendships and complex friendships. Simple friendships include "associates," who center their interaction around a particular interest such as golf or membership in club, church, or similar organization; "useful contacts," who are willing to help make connections and open doors, especially when it comes to job opportunities; "favor or neighborly friends," who usually live locally and are happy to lend household items or water plants without expecting to socialize; and "fun friends," who enjoy each other's company in many different social contexts but are "low-maintenance," in that they do not require deep conversations or obligations on either side.

Complex friendships, on the other hand, include "helpmates," or friends who socialize together, are essentially reliable, and help each other out in practical ways without being confidants; "comforters or rocks," who are friends that not only socialize and assist each other in practical ways, but also give each other emotional support; "confidants," who are trustworthy friends that may not live nearby but can share even the darkest of secrets, serve as reliable sounding boards, and provide emotional support; and "soulmates," who are friends that "confide, provide emotional support, help each other, and enjoy each other's company. Soulmates also share a similar outlook on life, feeling they are 'on the same wavelength.' They have a strong emotional bond, a high degree of commitment, and a keen sense of connection, of knowing each other 'inside out.'"

Whatever range of friends we have, there is an inherent moral dimension to friendship. For people to refer to themselves as "friends," especially "good friends" or "best friends," is a short-handed way of saying "We accept each other for who we are, we are loyal to each other, we wish each other the best, we help each other achieve success and happiness, and we trust each other enough to be honest, even critical, if we think it is in the other person's best interest."

▪ *Reflect on your friendships by listing the friends you've had over the years. Include anyone you consider a friend in some way.*

▪ *Using the descriptions of the different types of friendships listed above, draw a box around those friends who fall into the category of simple friendships—associates, useful contacts, favor or neighborly friends, and fun friends.*

▪ *Next, circle those who represent complex friendships—comforters or rocks, confidants, and soulmates.*

▪ *For those people whose names you circled, list the qualities of each that makes him or her important to you.*

▪ *What role does faith play in your friendships? What does each of your friends teach you about God's love and friendship?*

▪ *Now reflect on what kind of friend you are to others. Who would list you as a simple friend? A complex friend? What qualities do your friends value in you?*

▪ *Finally, reflect on your relationship with God. Do you consider God to be a simple friend or a complex friend in your life? What kind of friend would God describe you as?*

How might you nurture a richer relationship with God? In what ways would being better friends with God shape your existing friendships? How would it shape the way you make new friends?

8 Spiritual Exercise
The Practice of Practice

In theory there is no difference between theory and practice.
In practice there is.

—Yogi Berra

In our fast-paced lives, it's difficult enough to find time to exercise, let alone to get the results we want. The key, athletes teach us, is to be disciplined. Take Michael Jordan, for example. Despite his considerable God-given abilities, he put everything he had into each and every basketball practice. He wanted to amplify what he was naturally good at, but he also wanted to challenge himself to master those aspects of the game that he found difficult. He also worked closely with his coaches, ate right, and studied the game and its best players. As he later explained, he was able to set scoring records and win games at the buzzer, even when he was injured or ill, because his disciplined approach to the game allowed him to get into "the zone." His moves, passes, and shots were so ingrained in him through practice that they were instinctive, part of his nature.

Great athletes in sports from baseball to table tennis, football to swimming say the same thing: practicing certain disciplines over and over allows them to perform at their best, even in the worst conditions.

Just as our bodies require physical exercise, our souls require spiritual exercise to be healthy. In his letter to Timothy, St. Paul explains:

> Train yourself in godliness, for while physical training is of some value, godliness is valuable in every way, holding promise for both the present life and the life to come. The saying is sure and worthy of full acceptance. For to this end we toil and struggle, because we have our hope set on the living God.

Spirituality, then, is the discipline of putting our hope and trust in God. All other spiritual disciplines follow and can never be ends in themselves; they must always lead to a deeper, richer relationship with God. Richard Foster offers a helpful analogy:

> A farmer is helpless to grow grain; all he can do is provide the right conditions for the growing of grain. He cultivates the ground, he plants the seed, he waters the plants, and then

the natural forces of the earth take over and up comes the grain. This is the way it is with the Spiritual Disciplines— they are a way of sowing the Spirit. The Disciplines are God's way of getting us into the ground; they put us where he can work within us and transform us. By themselves the Spiritual Disciplines can do nothing; they can only get us to the place where something can be done. They are God's means of grace.

If our souls are the meeting ground between our human spirit and God's Spirit, then the more we condition our souls, the more receptive we are to God's grace. The purpose of spiritual disciplines is to help us condition our souls and to make us fertile ground for the seeds of faith.

Such talk of union with God and spiritual exercise may sound appealing in theory, but these concepts are meaningless unless they translate into reality and practice. As the quotation that opened this chapter suggests, theory and practice are at once interrelated and at odds. One the one hand, theory provides a goal and suggests a structure within which to meet that goal, while practice is where the real work of achieving the stated goal takes place. On the other hand, especially when it comes to philosophy and theology, theory often becomes so overemphasized that it trumps practice. As my father-in-law said to me when I first took up golf and bought every instruction manual I could get my hands on, "You can't learn golf from a book. You learn golf by golfing." The same is true in the spiritual life: you learn how to communicate with God by communicating with God.

In biblical times, the struggle between theory and practice, faith and spiritual disciplines was virtually nonexistent. People simply practiced solitude, worship, prayer, and celebration because these spiritual disciplines brought them into closer union with the God they wholeheartedly believed in. Today, we struggle with the very existence of God, let alone with the relevance and practicality of faith and spiritual disciplines. That the list of traditional Christian practices includes fasting, frugality, chastity, sacrifice, and submission doesn't exactly make spiritual disciplines overly appealing in today's world of instant gratification.

But practice wouldn't be practice if it were easy, if it didn't require trust and dedication, if it didn't help us grow and become stronger. The legendary baseball player Henry (Hank) Aaron once said of practice, "I don't see pitches down the middle anymore—not even in batting practice." Through practice, he eventually was able to hit fastballs without the slightest thought. So, he dedicated himself to practicing hitting curve balls, off-speed pitches, and sliders. Similarly, William James once advised, "Everybody should do at least two things each day that he hates to do, just for practice."

PRACTICE FOR SPIRITUAL GROWTH

As we prepare to move on to more overtly religious and spiritual practices in the next two sections of this book, the following six general disciplines might prove helpful in the long journey of faith.

1. Embrace the Journey

In the opening line of his best-selling book *The Road Less Traveled,* M. Scott Peck writes, "Life is difficult." Peck's point is to teach us that once we acknowledge that life is tough, we are free to *embrace* life to the fullest extent. We let go of misconceptions about what life owes us and grab onto the truth that life gives us what we put into it. We cease trying to control every aspect of life and begin opening ourselves to new possibilities and new ways of seeing things.

■ *Identify one practice that might help you better embrace your life's journey.*

2. Be Awake, Aware, and Alive

The art of seeking the something more in life—meaning and purpose—requires us to be awake, alert, and alive. It also requires us to be open, daring, and bold enough to think in new ways. Rather than seeking through other people's eyes and accepting at face value what they seek and discover, we must train ourselves to be skilled observers who seek and find in our own way. Of course, we have much to learn from others and we must always embrace our journeys in light of community, but it is crucial to believe that seeking is not only all right, it is essential to our lives.

■ *If Socrates had it right that the unexamined life is not worth living, how might you better practice the art of examining your own life so that you can live more fully?*

3. Log the Experience

As we sharpen our skills at embracing our spiritual journey and being mindful of how grace moves in our lives, it becomes increasingly important to take note of where we have been, where we are now, and where we are going. I call this "logging the experience."

Logging our spiritual experiences can be done in many ways. Some people keep a journal. Others compose music, paintings, or poetry. Others talk with a friend. Still others take photographs, dance, or sing to explore the inner landscape of the spirit. There is no right or wrong way to log the experience; the point is simply to do it. Taking time out of each day to reflect on life as it is happening is crucial for making continuity out of discontinuity and for seeing the larger tapestry of our relationships, jobs, free time, and lives.

■ *How might you better log your experiences in life?*

4. Seek Out Kindred Seekers and Mentors

Most successful athletes have a coach and teammates, friends, and rivals who push them to perform at their very best level. Why should we be reluctant to seek peers and mentors to help us get the most out of our lives?

■ *Who are the people who've taught you the most about life?*
■ *If you were to name someone who you think would be a good mentor, who would it be? Challenge yourself to ask that person to be your mentor.*

5. Live into Your Questions

When faced with the big questions of life—Where do we come from? Why are we here? Is there a God? Why do we suffer?—we can respond in many different ways. We can avoid such questions or, worse yet, be paralyzed by them. Or, we can face them—even if we do so slowly and carefully.

The German poet Rainer Maria Rilke wisely advises us to "live into our questions" as a way of embracing their energy. If we embrace the journey of life, if we are skilled observers, if we log our experiences along the way, and if we seek out kindred seekers and mentors, then we are much more open to living into our questions. As Rilke suggests, living into our questions means facing them and working through them.

■ *What are the most pressing questions at this time in your life? How might you better "live into them" and harness their energy for growth?*

6. Have Fun!

Religion and spirituality often get a bad rap as being heavy stuff for serious, somber people. Pondering ultimate meaning, struggling to find God or to help God find us, nurturing hope in the face of suffering, curbing our worldly appetites, going to church, reading the Bible, and living according to values and codes sound like all work and no play. And no matter how hard we work, it seems there is always more we can do and become. So why do we bother building a disciplined faith life rooted in Scripture and religion?

Quite simply, because faith is fun. In fact, to use religious language, it is joyful. The Bible is filled with stories of people whose faith not only saved them from utter despair but led them to sheer joy. Think of the joy of Abraham and Sarah when they learned that in their nineties they would bear a son named Isaac—whose name means "may God laugh"—and become the ancestors of all nations. Think of the joy of the Israelites when, after forty years in the wilderness with Moses, they were able to reclaim their homeland. Recall the joy of those who were healed by Jesus and ran to share the Good News. Imagine the joy of those, especially the marginalized, who ate, drank, and laughed with Jesus.

▨ *What do you find most joyful in life? What gets in the way of your joy? How might you overcome these obstacles? How can your faith help you enjoy life more?*

TWO **ROOTS**

*For the Church is like the trees in summer-time—
some boughs are covered in leaves, while others are
bare; and if the boughs are bare, you know the roots
of the tree are diseased.*
                    —William Langland

Introduction

At this stage in this book we stand at a crossroad between digging in the dirt of our lives to find seeds of faith and consciously nurturing these seeds so that they can take root and bear fruit in our daily lives.

Several summers ago, I learned just how important roots are. The branches on the tree outside my study window were dying, so I called a tree specialist. Within moments of his arrival, he declared, "Whatcha've got here is a dirty elm." Then, pointing to the other trees in my yard, he added, "These are all dirty elms. Too bad." After I asked him what he meant, he explained that when my house was built in the mid-fifties, it was common for builders to plant this type of elm tree because they grew to maturity and looked good very quickly. "The problem," he said, "is that as soon as they're grown, their roots are no good and they begin dying. Then they shed their bark and leaves all over the place until eventually you have to cut 'em down."

To offset the pain of lopping off branches for the time being, I went to our favorite garden center (which, interestingly, is named Gethsemane) to buy some trees to plant. After selecting a weeping Japanese maple and a multi-stem redbud to plant in front of the house and a Japanese maple for outside my study window, I asked the experts for their advice on how to properly plant the trees. "Dig the hole twice as wide and deep as the root-ball so the root system can grow easily," they said. "Then, add compost, black dirt, and Mycor Tree Saver."

As I hauled the trees home in my truck, it dawned on me that this whole experience illuminated the parable of the sower and provided a few new metaphors for understanding the nature of faith. The elms in my yard were like the faith that grows quickly but soon dies because it has a lousy root system. Or like the faith that looks good on the outside but is dying on the inside for lack of belief and practice. And the trees I was about to plant were akin to the seeds of faith we receive from God and, through thousands of years of growth, the Christian tradition.

As I began digging through the tough soil and old roots in my yard to make holes twice as big as the trees' root-balls, I realized that, when it comes to faith, I spend most of my energy trying to make God fit my life, rather than making room in my life for God to take root and grow.

It's been said that suffering carves spaces in us that God will fill if we don't race to do so ourselves. Likewise, joy and beauty, love and laughter expand our souls and make room for God if we rest in them, rather than letting anger or fear shrink our souls.

At the same time, just as guidance, nutrients, and disease-fighting agents were necessary in my preparation of the soil to feed the tree, essential ingredients such as spiritual mentors, Scripture, and Christian tradition are necessary in the ongoing work of feeding our faith.

The spiritual practices in this section—meditation, prayer, discipleship, worship, emulating spiritual heroes, spiritual direction, sacramentality, and celebration—will help us make room in our lives for God and nurture a healthy relationship with God that lasts a lifetime. They will help us be like trees in summertime, to borrow a line from William Langland, that are covered in leaves and bear fruit.

Happy planting!

Spiritual wisdom to consider as you develop your roots:

Wisdom is oftentimes nearer when we stoop than when we soar.
—William Wordsworth

Gardens are not created or made, they unfold—spiraling open like the silk petals of an evening primrose flower to reveal the ground plot of the mind and heart of the gardener and the good earth.
—Wendy Johnson

9 Listening for the Still Small Voice of God
The Practice of Meditation

Christian meditation, very simply, is the ability to hear God's voice and obey his word. It is that simple. I wish I could make it more complicated for those who like things difficult. It involves no hidden mysteries, no secret mantras, no mental gymnastics, no esoteric flights into the cosmic consciousness. The truth of the matter is that the great God of the universe, the Creator of all things desires our fellowship.
—Richard Foster

REFLECTION

John H. White, a Pulitzer Prize–winning photographer for the Chicago *Sun-Times* and a devout Christian, begins each day the same way: he arises in the darkness of the early morning and drives to the shores of Lake Michigan to photograph the day's first light. "It is my meditation, my time with God," he says. "To capture each day the moment it begins helps me to appreciate life as a gift and to focus my attention on making the most out of each and every day." Soon after he finishes his meditation, John dives into the often-stressful, always action-packed job of photographing a day in the life of the city—from fires and auto accidents to parades and portraits. Beloved for his peaceful manner and gift of seeing deeply into the world around him, John finishes all of his conversations with people by saying, "Keep in flight."

I tell you about John because he is a master practitioner of meditation. And not just any meditation, but a meditation deeply rooted in Scripture and Christian tradition as well as day-to-day life. John embodies what it means to live life with the Bible in one hand and a newspaper in the other. He is disciplined and keeps his focus on what matters even when he is at his busiest. While he may not have a photo of God, his portfolio provides a stunning portrait of God at work in the world and in John's life.

From the Psalms to the Gospels, the practice of meditation is referred to many times in Scripture. The psalmist proclaims: "I will call to mind the deeds of the LORD; I will remember your wonders of old. I will meditate on all your work, and muse on your mighty deeds. Your way, O God, is holy. What god is so great as our God? You are the God who works wonders; you have displayed your might among the peoples." The Gospel writers tell us that in the midst of his busy ministry, Jesus "withdrew ... to a deserted place by himself," "went out to the mountain to pray," and "spent the night in prayer to God."

What these passages teach us is that the practice of meditation allows us to connect to God in an intimate way, and from that connection we learn how to live our lives fully, in tune with our divine purpose. For Jesus, silence and solitude were essential practices that enabled him to talk to God, to discern and accept his mission on earth, and to muster up the energy he needed to serve others when he was most tired or filled with doubt. While it would be enough to observe and follow Jesus' example, he extends the invitation to the disciples and, disciples need all of us to "come away to a deserted place all by yourselves and rest a while."

Since biblical times, many have accepted Jesus' invitation to meditate as a way to get to know God—John the apostle in the first century, the desert fathers and mothers in the fourth century, the Benedictines in the sixth century, and luminaries like Thérèse of Lisieux, Thomas Merton, and Henri Nouwen. At its foundation, meditation is the practice of being in friendship with God. Beyond dogma and doctrine, beyond heady statements *about* God, meditation puts us in direct contact *with* God. In meditation, we come to the quiet and listen for the "still small voice of God" at work in the world and in each of us. Or, as the Russian mystic Theophan the Recluse put it, we meditate "to descend with the mind into the heart, and there to stand before the face of the Lord, ever-present, all seeing, within you."

More than 1,500 years ago, Benedict of Nursia, Italy, wrote the *Rule* to guide the life and prayer of members of the order he founded, the Benedictines. All these years later, the *Rule* is a remarkable document that reveals how one can, and should, seek God, who seeks us first. Benedict did not separate the inner from the outer, the sacred from the secular, the material from the spiritual. Rather, he taught that God can be found in silence and in the timeline of the day. There is nowhere that God is not.

After opening the *Rule* with the provocative words, "Listen carefully, my [child] . . . and attend with the ear of your heart," Benedict offers lessons on how to pray alone and in community. In Benedict's time, monks gathered seven times a day to pray the Liturgy of the Hours, which includes Scripture, hymns, biblical commentaries, and prayers. Additionally, they spent two to three hours per day practicing *lectio divina,* or "meditative, prayerful reading." The practice of *lectio divina* consists of four interrelated practices: *lectio* (reading), *meditatio* (pondering), *oratio* (praying), and *contemplatio* (resting in God).

To begin, we slowly and reflectively read a chosen spiritual text (typically a Bible passage). Next, we ponder words, images, and insights that strike us. Then, we pray to God whatever is in our hearts—thanksgiving, repentance, hope, need, and so on. Finally, we "rest in God" or "pray without words" by simply being and feeling God's loving presence in our lives.

While meditation and *lectio divina* have been essential elements in the lives of biblical figures, saints, and holy people through the ages, we can't help wondering if these disciplines are even possible for us to practice today. I know as I race around in the morning to get the kids and myself ready for the day, fight traffic, work all day, fight traffic again, pick the kids up, help with dinner, read to and prepare the kids for bed, and try to share time with my wife, I wonder: "Seriously! Can any of us become contemplatives in the midst of our busy, noisy lives?"

In her book *Simple Ways to Pray,* which brings the practice of *lectio divina* to life in very accessible ways, Emilie Griffin offers the answer: yes. She explains that when she was first introduced to meditation through reading Thomas Merton, she had no idea what she was doing. "I simply followed the advice I had been given: put yourself in the presence of God." In those days, she says, "my life was hectic. I was living in New York City, going back and forth to work on the subway, traveling to business meetings frequently by air, and at the same time trying to be a good wife and a good mother to three small children. . . . Anxiety was my middle name. It's no wonder I needed prayer." Eventually, she began seeking silence and solitude. Sometimes she'd go on a retreat to spend time with God and pray with Scripture. She developed the practice of Eucharistic adoration and talking to God. "When I couldn't go to a retreat house," she says, "I would go into any open Catholic church where the Blessed Sacrament was reserved for prayer in the tabernacle . . . or else I would look for a 'vest pocket' park (you can find them in Manhattan, small parks on city streets, maybe with a waterfall) or bench in an atrium or public place (a library, a coffeehouse) where I could come to the quiet." Sometimes she got up very early and watched the sun come up as she listened to the birds chirp and thanked God for the day.

By "stumbling" into silence, Griffin took the first steps to becoming a contemplative in the modern world. "In contemplative prayer God is infusing us with his love and grace," Griffin writes. "It is not what we do but what God does in us." Our job is to be open to God's grace, most especially when we are busy.

To practice contemplation and meditation, we don't have to live a cloistered lifestyle. We simply have to be aware of God's presence wherever we are. This way, we join John White in seeing God in sunrises, and Benedict in hearing God with the ears of our hearts, and Emilie Griffin in experiencing God's grace in city parks. What do you see and hear when you come to the quiet?

PRACTICE FOR SPIRITUAL GROWTH

MEDITATION

Meditation is not about separating the praying self from the everyday self. And it is not about becoming extreme ascetics, replacing thoughtful faith with blind piety, or cutting ourselves off from community to build a "Jesus and me" relationship. Meditation, as Thomas Merton put it, "has no point and no reality unless it is firmly rooted in *life*." Meditation, therefore, is the practice of forming a deep engagement with the world and coming to see God at work in everything. It's about tapping into what Thomas Merton called the "hidden wholeness" that exists in each of us.

In his book *Streams of Living Water*, Richard Foster offers many helpful suggestions for practicing meditation in everyday life; I include some of them here.

■ *First, experiment with varied venues for solitude. Take a predawn walk, listening to the awakening sounds of your world. Limit your speaking for one day and see what you learn about yourself and others. Observe others in an airport or bus station and reflect on what you see. Take a one-day, three-day, or seven-day silent retreat. For one month, leave your car radio off and make your morning commute a mini-retreat.*

■ *Second, try praying with Scripture using* lectio divina *(described in detail below).*

■ *Third, practice "holy leisure." Take a nap. Spend an hour visiting with your neighbor about nothing important. Watch the sun go down. Take a walk, not for exercise or to study plant life, but for the sheer joy of walking. Sit in silence; do nothing.*

PREPARING FOR *LECTIO DIVINA*

The goal of *lectio divina* is to "listen with the ear of our heart" for the voice of God, to lose ourselves in God's love and find our deepest identity in God, and to awaken to God's presence in everything. But the reality is that the effects of *lectio divina* will probably be subtle and not dramatic. Benedictine sister Katherine Kraft advises, "If we approach *lectio* in faith, as a way of encountering God by means of a sacred text, when the time in *lectio* feels unproductive, as it often will when God is silent, we will be able to accept that experience with equanimity, content with simply being there, open and receptive." *Lectio divina* is a practice that requires discipline and patience. Over time, we begin to notice that we are less anxious and harried, we are hopeful rather than cynical, and we are more sensitively aware of the needs of others. Eventually, we experience a deeper understanding of Scripture, the revealed Word of God, and connection to God.

- *Unlike the monks of Benedict's time, we aren't able to pray the Liturgy of the Hours seven times a day and practice lectio divina for another two to three hours! Even contemporary Benedictines have adapted the Rule and gather three times each day (morning, noon, and evening) for common prayer and practice lectio divina for an hour or so. But, still, we likely don't have that kind of time either. So, you may wish to set aside fifteen to thirty minutes a day for lectio divina.*

- *Pick a fixed time of day when you can be silent and undisturbed. Some people prefer the morning and discipline themselves to get up a little earlier than usual to meditate and pray to set the tone for the day. If you're anything like me, mornings are too chaotic and evenings instead provide a quiet time to pray, review the day, and prepare for the next day.*

- *Choose a quiet place where you can sit comfortably, attentively, and prayerfully. It's best if you can choose a place that you can dedicate exclusively to prayer, so that upon entering this space you naturally transition into a prayerful mode.*

- *Decide what your lectio text will be in advance. Some people follow the daily Mass readings, while others work their way through the books of the Bible or through the chapters of a spiritual book. I use the monthly publication Magnificat, Phyllis Tickle's three-volume book The Divine Hours, and the Nineteenth Annotation of St. Ignatius of Loyola's Spiritual Exercises for my lectio divina prayer time.*

■ *Place yourself gently in God's presence and let go of all thoughts, especially worries and stresses.*

■ *Ask for the grace to better understand the text and form a stronger connection to God.*

■ *Finally, name what it is you most want from this session of* lectio divina.

PRACTICING *LECTIO DIVINA*

■ Lectio *(Reading): Read the chosen text reflectively and slowly. Enter into it as deeply as you can. Reread all or part of the text several times. If it helps, read aloud. Stop when a particular word, phrase, or image strikes you.*

■ Meditatio *(Pondering): Stay with whatever touches you. Ponder and savor it, letting it penetrate your awareness, mind, and heart.*

■ Oratio *(Praying): As you ponder, a prayer of thanks, repentance, need, or love may emerge. Allow yourself to express your prayer. Take as long as you need. What is it you seek most in life right now? What do you most want to say to God? What do you most want to hear from God?*

■ Contemplatio *(Resting in God): At times, your prayer moves beyond words and images. When this happens, you are "resting in God." Let yourself trust enough to yield to the moment. As the sense of resting ceases, return to reading the text and let the rhythm of reading, pondering, praying, and resting in God play itself out naturally and fluidly.*

■ *End each time of* lectio divina *with a prayer, such as the Lord's Prayer.*

10 Lord, Teach Us to Pray
The Practice of Prayer

Pray without ceasing.
—St. Paul, 1 Thessalonians 5:17

REFLECTION

When I asked a friend of mine who is a popular spiritual director what people most struggle with in their faith lives, he immediately responded, "Prayer." "Why?" I asked. "Because deep down, most people feel like they don't know how to pray, or that they pray incorrectly. I meet with bishops, priests, nuns, parents, everyday people in the pews, college kids—you name it. Invariably, they want to know how to pray and how they can tell if they're doing it right."

The question of how to pray is hardly new. As the Gospel stories reveal, even Jesus had to learn from his parents and community how to worship, study the Torah, and pray. Eventually, through intense prayer, Jesus came to understand who he really was, and formed an intimate relationship with God. From this place of prayer-connection, he remained strong and centered even when the demands on him were at their greatest—to heal, to feed, to teach, to forgive, to love, to lead. Time and again, he retreated to a quiet place to pray and listen and be restored so that he could be the best servant possible.

Though they had prayed all their lives as good Jewish believers, the disciples saw something different in Jesus' prayer. As Wayne Muller explains, They felt something different in the way he touched, the way he spoke, the way he listened, and waited, and remained at peace. When they saw him with the poor, with the hungry, with the lame and the lepers, he was so calm, so kind, so unafraid. They wanted to feel what Jesus felt. They wanted to be that clear, that whole. They wanted to feel his peace and wisdom in their own hearts and minds. And so they asked him, "Lord, teach us to pray." Jesus responded by giving them these words:

Our Father,
who art in heaven,
Hallowed be thy name.
Thy Kingdom come,
thy will be done,
on earth, as it is in heaven.
Give us this day our daily bread.

And forgive us our trespasses,
as we forgive those who trespass against us.
And lead us not into temptation,
but deliver us from evil.

What is most striking about this exchange between the disciples and Jesus is that they did not ask him for a specific prayer—they asked him *how* to pray. The Our Father is not a prayer to be memorized and repeated mindlessly. It's a guide on how to practice prayer and how to talk with God.

The whole point of prayer is to form a relationship with God that is so intimate we dare call him "Father" (Abba) and to think of ourselves as an integral part of the human family. When we pray, we connect on a very deep level with God the Creator and with all of creation. Quite simply, we are not self-sufficient. We need God, and we need each other. Again, Wayne Muller puts it well:

Every day there are moments when I find myself drawn to pray. I pray because I must, because regardless of my good intentions I lose my bearings. I make mistakes. I am stopped by the way the world changes and confounds my plans. When a loved one is beset by illness, ache, or fear, I pray their healing may be deep and true. When I feel suddenly lost or lonely, I pray for the comfort of a nourishing spirit that will teach me, show me the way. At other times my prayer is filled with gratefulness for the numberless blessings showered on my life. In these moments, my prayer is astonishingly simple: *Thank you.*

Other lessons from the Lord's Prayer abound: The God "who art in heaven" is closer to us than we are to ourselves. God is both transcendent and immanent, wholly other and intimately near. At the same time, heaven is not so much a geographical or celestial location "up there" as it is a state of the heart "in here," by which we recognize God at work in the world around us. The Our Father teaches us to honor God's name by praying, being grateful for "our daily bread," aligning our will with God's, seeking God's forgiveness and forgiving others, and resisting temptations that lure us away from what is good and right.

At its most basic level, the practice of prayer is communication with God. Christians hold that the initiative comes from God, who moves people to pray and who listens and responds to our prayers. Most of us are familiar with various types of prayer—petition, intercession, thanksgiving, repentance, adoration, and praise. No matter what the type, true prayer is not about reciting formulaic words; it's about expressing what's in our hearts. Many of us are afraid to pray because we feel we're unworthy or don't have the right words. Others of us aren't sure God is really listening, or we don't trust that God will do anything even if God is listening. Some of us are afraid that God might actually be listening and will respond in ways that might surprise us or make demands on us.

In my own life, one key experience has helped me better understand the nature and practice of prayer. Early in our marriage, my wife, Liz, and I were invited by a group of Cistercian monks to speak at a small conference of their vocation directors at their monastery in Snowmass, Colorado.

Not surprisingly, the vocation directors and abbots we met were extremely well read and wise. Session after session they listened to our presentations and pressed us with questions about the concerns of young people today. They were not looking for recruiting plans or ways to conform their monastery to the modern world. All they wanted was a dialogue about young people today so they could be better equipped to welcome any young person who might approach them to discern a vocation to their order. In exchange, they shared with us a privileged glimpse into the monastic way of life.

The rhythm of life at the monastery was more about being than doing; it was about connecting with creation and savoring life. In the mornings we'd arise and sit on the porch of our stone hermitage overlooking oceans of grass that the monks rented out to cattle ranchers to feed livestock. The sun would emerge from the blue sky and bounce off the dewy ground back into the thin air from which it came. Far in the distance, the church bells would call the monks to the second round of their morning prayers at Terce, or 6:00 AM; amazingly, they'd already prayed once, at Prime, or 3:00 AM, while we slept.

We'd shower, dress, gather our notes, and walk down the hill to the retreat center, which was hand hewn by monks according to the strictest monastic standards and thus was meant to stand the toughest tests of time. We'd eat a simple breakfast with the monks over quiet conversation and then spend the morning lecturing and listening. For lunch, we'd walk to the cloister where the monks lived, ate, and prayed.

The monk assigned to read aloud that week as the others ate in silence would pick up where he'd left off the day before and continue until the end of the meal, then he'd climb down from the loft and eat his lunch as we headed back to the conference center for more dialogue. In the evening we would eat together. At night, Liz and I would sit on the front porch of our hermitage and discuss the day under the brightest stars we've ever seen.

The combination of living, albeit for a brief while, within the rhythms of the monastery while listening day after day to the monks explain their vocation of prayer both enlightened and confounded us. Over and over we'd ask, "But what does your life of prayer *do*?" They'd respond, "we aren't here to *do* anything. We are here to pray." They explained that at the core of monasticism is the belief that God listens to prayers, so the more they prayed for the well-being of humanity, the better for everyone. They were responding to a call—the call to pray.

At the end of a very holy experience with the monks, Liz and I left feeling both filled and unrequited. We'd prayed. We'd witnessed prayer by people who had devoted their lives to prayer and had abandoned other callings such as painting or writing or other ways of life. And yet we struggled with whether prayer alone was a legitimate vocation—what about all the injustice in the world? We also struggled with whether God really does listen to prayer—what about all the needs of people who don't pray or don't have anyone praying specifically for them?

I think often of those monks and their prayer. And over time I've come to see that that very question is the point. The monks are a special witness to how humans can react to the mystery of life, to the questions of why we are here and how we are to respond to our Creator. In this age of achievement and ever-evolving technology, we send and receive signals and pulses of information to and from outer space. We tune in to the radio and television transmissions that fill the air. And yet, all over the world monks and prayerful people send and receive signals into the great beyond that communicate with God. Perhaps these are the transmissions that really matter most.

PRACTICE FOR SPIRITUAL GROWTH

Prayer is the most central of the spiritual disciples. Disciplines such as seeking, solitude, study, and meditation are integral parts of a mature spiritual life and certainly enhance prayer, but it is the practice of prayer that puts us into direct relationship with God. In prayer, we are invited to "be still and know that I am God." And in prayer, God meets us wherever we are and draws us into deeper understandings about the meaning of life, love, and service.

Christians hold that prayer is a two-way street; God responds to our prayers, and we respond to God through prayer. Christians also hold that prayer is something we learn.

■ *Think about your own experience of prayer. Who first taught you how to pray? How do you pray today? Do you recite traditional prayers, pray spontaneously, or both? Whether you pray regularly or infrequently, what do you find most difficult about prayer? What inhibits you? What do you find easiest about prayer? What inspires you to pray?*

▪ *Now, think about what you expect to come from your prayer. Do you seek overt or subtle signs that God is listening and responding? List experiences in which you've felt your prayers have been answered and in which they seem to have gone unanswered.*

▪ *Fundamentally, prayer is about learning how to follow God individually and as part of the human community. It's important to realize that we never pray alone. God is always with us, as are all the holy women and men throughout history who have been pray-ers. The fruit of the Spirit found in prayer is love, joy, peace, patience, kindness, generosity, faithfulness, gentleness, and self-control, and freedom from selfishness, anger, and greed.*

▪ *Reflect on how you might enhance your prayer life. You might seek the guidance of someone you trust and respect for the depth of their prayer life (see chapter 14), read a good book on the practice of prayer, make a booklet of your favorite traditional prayers, write some of your own prayers, go to church more regularly, or volunteer to serve those in the greatest need and then reflect on the experience.*

▪ *As a spiritual discipline, prayer requires structure and regularity. When you feel ready, devote one month to praying regularly and tracing the effect it has on your faith, your understanding of God, and your daily outlook on life. Set aside a specific time and place in which you can devote at least ten minutes per day to prayer. Light a candle or make the sign of the cross to help you transition into a space of prayer.*

■ *Begin by clearing your mind and allowing yourself to be still. Quietly ask yourself: What's in my heart in this moment? In what ways did I sense God's presence or absence today? In what ways was I at my best today? In what ways was I at my worst? What grace do I most want for myself? For others? Conclude with the Our Father or another traditional prayer. As time goes on, it might help to practice* lectio divina *with a Scripture passage or excerpt from a book of spirituality.*

■ *Take a moment to notice how you felt as you prayed. What held your attention? Were you distracted or free? What, if any, experience of God did you have? What do you hope to do better tomorrow and in the days ahead?*

11 Faith Seeking Understanding
The Practice of Thinking

Live the questions now. Perhaps you will then gradually,
without noticing it, live along some distant day into the
answer.

—Rainer Maria Rilke

REFLECTION

Any good gardener is also a thinker. She studies what each item in her garden needs to flourish, and she plans accordingly. She reads manuals and books, talks to other gardeners and experts, tests different theories, and makes the necessary adjustments year after year.

It's similar in the faith life. Anyone serious about growing her faith is also a thinker. She knows that faith and reason go hand in hand, and so studies Scripture, history, Christian tradition, theology, philosophy, science, art, and music. She prays and worships in community, talks about faith with mentors and fellow believers, and ponders God's presence and will. At various times, she is called to consider arguments against her faith or is asked to explain—even to defend— her faith.

Challenges to Scripture stories and tenets of the faith abound. Consider, for example, a 2006 *Washington Post* story by Alan Cooperman titled "Researchers Break Ice on Jesus 'Miracle.'" The article explains that after combining evidence of a cold snap 2,000 years ago with sophisticated mapping of the Sea of Galilee, Israeli and U.S. scientists were able to determine that Jesus did not walk on water, as the New Testament indicates, but instead walked on floating ice. While the Sea of Galilee has never frozen in modern times, the scientists argue that, based on geological core samples, there were at least two cold spells in the region some 1,500 and 2,500 years ago that could have produced ice floats substantial enough for a person to walk on. To the average eye, especially in bad weather, someone walking on the ice would have appeared to be walking on water.

One of the scientists from the study, Doron Nof, an Israeli professor of oceanography at Florida State University, has also argued elsewhere that "strong winds across the narrow, shallow Gulf of Suez could have lowered the Red Sea by ten feet, allowing the Israelites to cross to safety and then swallowing up an Egyptian army within a few minutes when the wind stopped, just as the book of Exodus says." While other scientists in recent years have explained Noah's flood as simply seawater surging from the Mediterranean into the Black Sea from glacial melting, and Joshua's destruction of the walls of Jericho as the work of an earthquake, Nof qualifies his findings by saying, "This isn't going to convince a believer not to believe, and nobody's trying to do that. At least, I'm not trying to do that. I personally believe that all these biblical stories are based on some truth."

What impact do arguments against or scientific explanations of Scripture stories, faith claims, and miracles have on your relationship to God? To Scripture? To organized religion? What effect do they have on your religious practice and outward expression of faith? Do you believe that science and religion are at odds? That faith is a leap *over* science and reason?

It's commonly held that science and religion, reason and faith, have always been at war over the truth. Worse, many people believe that science is about provable truth, while religion belongs to the realm of fantasy and superstition. Simply put, they believe that religion is for people who don't think, let alone study science.

But as historians have revealed, the reality is that the realms of science and religion have been deeply intertwined for most of history. From the Middle Ages to the nineteenth century, most people in the Western world believed that God wrote the two "books" of nature and Scripture, and that it was important to explore both.

While Christian Europe turned away from scientific thinking in the Middle Ages, Muslim scholars continued to explore the fields of science, mathematics, and astronomy. Their work was later read and absorbed by Christian monks, theologians, and believers such as Roger Bacon, Nicholas of Cusa, Nicolaus

Copernicus, Johannes Kepler, and Isaac Newton. It wasn't until the eighteenth century that science and religion were separated into distinct disciplines. Even then, they were not considered to be at war over the truth. The battle between science and religion erupted when Charles Darwin published his work on evolution in the mid-nineteenth century. Yet many people, including clergy, still believed that science and religion were not at odds; they believed science and religion worked together to explain the how and why of creation.

Believers hold that God is knowable in two distinct ways: by faith and by reason. The practice of thinking, then, entails studying God's two books—the revelation and witness contained in Scripture and the tradition of the believing community throughout history, and the physical universe. Saint Anselm of Canterbury (1033–1109) described Christianity as "faith seeking understanding." He taught that, once they had accepted the gift of faith, it was wrong for Christians not to demonstrate by reason the truth of their belief. For Anselm, one begins in faith and then applies reason to inform that faith.

A burning question today is whether or not faith can inform reason. Quite simply, the answer is yes, for the great lesson of faith is that no matter how incredible our minds are, we humans are limited in our ability to know. Consequently, faith teaches us that we must approach both God and scientific discovery with humility, awe, and even reverence. This way, we open ourselves up to the possibilities of learning from other traditions, scrutinizing our own conclusions, and being creative in our search for truth.

To be a believer is to be a thinker. Christianity has a two-thousand-year history of grappling with the problems of human psychology, social organization, political power, and aesthetic imagination, of thinking and writing by some enormously gifted people, including at least two individuals, Augustine and Aquinas, who rank among the most profound, prolific, and creative minds of all eras." It embraces a sacramental principle that explores the natural world and elements of culture as vehicles through which God mediates grace to human beings. It embraces believers from all over the world and strives to be a universal, inclusive church that bridges gaps. And it emphasizes the importance of being a community that searches together for truth, meaning, and salvation.

PRACTICE FOR SPIRITUAL GROWTH

The practice of using your mind is a vital component of a healthy life and a healthy faith. Through thinking and attentive study, we train our minds to engage with, analyze, and interpret the seen and the unseen all around us.

Before we jump to the question of what to study, let's take a moment to discuss how to study. In his book *Celebration of Discipline,* Richard Foster offers the following four steps for practicing the discipline of study:

1 Repetition. The practice of memorizing and repeating lines from a book, a speech, or Scripture text helps to sharpen our minds and instill habits of thought that

make us more receptive to allowing what we learn to shape our behavior.

2 Concentration. In addition to bringing the mind repeatedly to the subject matter, concentrating our mental energies on that which we are studying makes us more likely to absorb and retain our subject. The human brain has a remarkable capacity to concentrate if we free it from distractions.

3 Comprehension. By repeatedly focusing our minds in a particular direction and concentrating on our chosen subject, we begin to better understand what we are studying. Comprehension then leads to insight.

4 Reflection. By reflecting on the meaning and significance of what we are studying, we come to understand not only our subject matter, but ourselves.

———————————

■ *Keeping these principles in mind, create a plan for practicing the discipline of study. Choose a week or, better yet, a month in which you can regularly focus your attention and think. The goal here is to make study a regular part of your life, especially when it comes to your faith.*

■ *God's two "books" are Scripture and nature. While you may be drawn to both, it would be most helpful to begin with Scripture. You might take a single book of the Bible and work your way through one segment at a time during each of your study sessions. Or, if it is a short book, you might read it straight through each time you sit down to study.*

■ *You may wish to read related books and Bible commentaries, reflect on experiences that help you understand and interpret what you are studying, and discuss what you are studying with others. If you can, take a Scripture course or go on a guided retreat.*

■ *In addition to studying Scripture, select a spiritual book that has been highly recommended. Choose a book of manageable size. Scan through it to get a feel for what the book covers, then read it slowly and carefully. You may find it helpful to keep a journal of ideas or questions the book raises for you.*

■ *You could also study a prayer or doctrine of the faith. A good place to start might be with the Nicene Creed. Using the method of lectio divina (outlined in chapter 9), ask yourself what elements of the creed do I wholeheartedly believe in? What gives me pause or is hard for me to understand? What do I have trouble believing, and why? What can I do to better understand and interpret the creed?*

After spending time with Scripture, turn your attention to God's other "book," the natural world. The poet Gerard Manley Hopkins maintained that we could contemplate God by contemplating the beauty and intricacy of a leaf.

■ *Set aside a regular time to take a walk through a park or the woods and observe everything you can. Study those things that you know little about—from moss to flowers to birds. What do they teach you about beauty? About God?*

As Richard Foster suggests, it also helps to study ourselves and others.

■ *What drives us, as humans? What controls us?*
■ *How do we behave toward each other?*
■ *How might we live deeper, richer lives?*
■ *Where is God in the interplay between humans?*

Finally, when it comes to studying our faith, it's helpful to heed the advice of C.S. Lewis:

There are certain things in Christianity that can be understood from the outside, before you have become a Christian. But there are a great many things that cannot be understood until after you have gone a certain distance along the Christian road. . . . Whenever you find any statement in Christian writings which you can make nothing of, do not worry. Leave it alone. There will come a day, perhaps years later, when you suddenly see what it meant. If one could understand it now, it would only do one harm."

12 Touchstones of the Sacred
The Practice of Living Sacramentally

The world is charged with the grandeur of God.
—Gerard Manley Hopkins, SJ

REFLECTION

At face value, waiting for someone at the airport and shopping for a greeting card are nice gestures. Through the lens of faith, they're sacramental moments filled with meaning and mystery.

Consider how you feel and what goes through your mind as you wait for a loved one to arrive from a trip, or as you browse greeting cards till you find just the right one for a friend. You consider the other person's qualities, his or her significance in your life, what your time together or the card's message will mean to each of you. Sometimes such waiting or browsing gives rise to other thoughts—about the meaning of life and friendship and love.

It's at this deeper level that waiting in an airport or browsing greeting cards become touchstones of the sacred. "A sacrament is when something holy happens," writes Frederick Buechner in his book *Wishful Thinking*. "It is transparent time, time which you can see through to something deep inside."

In the Christian tradition, Protestants and Catholics alike name specific sacraments that unfailingly serve as "outward signs, instituted by Christ, to give grace." Official Protestant sacraments include the Lord's Supper and baptism, while official Catholic sacraments name these plus five more: confirmation, reconciliation, anointing of the sick, marriage, and holy orders. "In other words," explains Buechner, "at such milestone moments as seeing a baby baptized or being baptized yourself, confessing your sins, getting married, dying, you are apt to catch a glimpse of the almost unbearable preciousness and mystery of life."

By practicing the sacraments and worshiping God in community at the Lord's table, we are being prepared week after week for the liturgy of our lives. Living sacramentally means seeking God in all things, sanctifying moments in time through prayer and meditation, kneeling in humility, enjoying family and friends, and celebrating life. It's the practice of turning our tables and meals into altars and Eucharistic acts of thanksgiving that welcome the stranger and those in need.

If the poet Gerard Manley Hopkins is right when he says "the world is charged with the grandeur of God," then the practice of living sacramentally is the practice of seeing God at work in the world. In Scripture we encounter many stories of what it means to see with faith eyes. Throughout his ministry, Jesus healed those who were physically and spiritually blind. Time and again he shows us that believing and seeing are paths to each other—seeing leads to believing, and believing leads to seeing. He also shows us that seeing with the eyes of faith is often a gradual process, and that we sometimes have to convince others that what we see is real by standing firm in our faith.

Of the many expressions of sacramental Christianity in music, architecture, art, literature, and science, one of my favorites is a book of essays called *Meditations from a Movable Chair* by the late author Andre Dubus. Each essay is a poignant testimonial to the power of faith by a man who lived passionately but suffered greatly after losing the use of his legs when he was hit by a car after pulling to the side of the road to help a stranded young couple.

In the essay "Sacraments," Dubus explains that because he is divorced, he cherishes all the more his visits with his young daughters, who live with their mother. On Tuesdays he drives his van with special hand controls to the girls' school to pick them up and take them home. Because they do not like the school lunches and are not allowed to bring their own, they are often hungry after school. Being a loving dad, Dubus brings them sandwiches, potato chips, soda, and Reese's peanut butter cups.

As he describes the arduous process of negotiating his wheelchair in his small kitchen to make sandwiches for his daughters, Dubus meditates on the sacramental quality of what he is doing. For him, the physical and emotional pain of not having his legs and of not being able to move around as easily as he once did is transformed into the very essence of what makes his time with his daughters and this task of making lunches so sacred. "On Tuesdays, when I make lunch for my girls," he says,

> I focus on this: the sandwiches are sacraments. Not the miracle of transubstantiation, but certainly parallel with it, moving in the same direction. If I could give my children my body to eat, again and again without losing it, my body like the loaves and fishes going endlessly into mouths and stomachs, I would do it. And each motion is a sacrament, this holding of plastic bags, of knives, of bread, of cutting board, this pushing of the chair, this spreading of mustard on bread, this trimming of liverwurst, of ham. All sacraments, as putting the lunches into a zippered bag is, and going down my six ramps to my car is. I drive on the highway, to the girls' town, to their school, and this is not simply a transition; it is my love moving by car from a place where my girls are not to a place where they are; even if I do not feel or acknowledge it, this is a sacrament.

Dubus goes on to say that if he were "much wiser, and much more patient, and had much greater concentration," he could sit in silence in his chair, look out his windows at a green tree and the blue sky, and know that "breathing is a gift; that a breath is sufficient for the moment; and that breathing air is breathing God." This is what it means to be sacramental.

The practice of living sacramentally is not merely about recognizing God in what we see, smell, touch, taste, and hear. It's about being a living sacrament of God ourselves—in our homes, places of work, neighborhoods, churches, and communities. Living sacramentally means loving others, spreading peace and joy, being decent and ethical, forgiving and seeking forgiveness, fighting for the rights of others, caring for the earth, and serving those in the greatest need.

PRACTICE FOR SPIRITUAL GROWTH

Richard Foster highlights seven strengths of the incarnational, sacramental tradition, which are summarized below. For each, identify how you might live more sacramentally, both in how you recognize God at work in the world and how you bring God into the world. Make a list and hold yourself accountable for making the necessary changes in your life that will lead to a more sacramental way of being.

The sacramental tradition . . .

1 underscores the fact that God is not distant but is truly among us right here, right now on this earth.

2 roots us in everyday life by recognizing God in the messiness and the mundane details of our lives.

3 gives meaning to our work by giving us a sense of calling, responsibility, freedom, creativity, dignity, community, solidarity with the poor, meaning, and purpose.

4 saves us from believing that spiritual things are wholly good and material things are wholly bad.

5 reminds us that we are made in the image and likeness of God.

6 makes of our body a portable sanctuary through which we experience God's presence and work in cooperation with God to make the world a better place.

7 deepens our ecological sensitivities by helping us grow in our stewardship of the earth.

———————————

What liturgies of life did you grow up with? For my family, mealtime was sacred, and we ate together, no matter what. Of course, there were times when one or more of us were in a rush or did not feel much like talking. But most evenings, we enjoyed coming together, talking about our day, telling stories, laughing, and even discussing difficult topics in our family or in the news.

- *What other practices can you think of to live more sacramentally?*

- *Terry Hershey explains that most of us would benefit from creating little liturgies that give us permission to transition into sacred time. For example, when you come home, instead of vegging out, take a deep breath and then play with your kids. Make date nights with your significant other. Sign up for a regular volunteer night at the local soup kitchen.*

- *Set aside a place and time in the evening to collect yourself and reflect on your day and your life. Sit in your favorite chair, light a candle, and give yourself permission to transition. Letting go of your worries and entering fully into the moment is a powerful form of worship in the liturgy of life.*

13 Marching with the Saints
The Practice of Being Fully Alive

For me to be a saint means to be myself.
—Thomas Merton

Growing up, stories of the saints did nothing for me. In Catholic grade school, the stories of martyrs who died for the faith or pious holy women and men who lived ascetic lives, prayed ceaselessly, and performed miracles were about as exciting as the statues of saints that stared down at us in plastered perfection from the church rafters. No matter how hard our teachers tried to convince us that the saints are holy women and men who model for us what it looks like to be fully alive and fully in touch with God, they just never seemed real enough to bother with.

Years later, when I moved to Chicago and became a parishioner at Old St. Patrick's, I had to reckon with the saints again. Not only did a huge statue of St. Patrick himself stare at me from the center of the sanctuary each week, but the parishioners, many of them Irish, went around invoking the saints like they were old friends.

Around that time, the church (which was built in 1846 and is the oldest public building in the city) was in the process of restoring to its original glory the beautiful Celtic stained glass and stenciling created in the early 1900s by renowned Irish artist Thomas Augustin O'Shaughnessy. During the restoration, I noticed that the niche along the north wall closest to the sanctuary was empty. After a quick survey, I confirmed that all of the other niches had statues of North American saints, such as Mother Cabrini, Martin de Porres, and Kateri Tekakwitha; I figured that one of the saints was getting a makeover. Then one Sunday I heard someone ask a parishioner why a saint was missing from the niche. "Oh, no statue is missing," she said, "We leave it open so people can imagine their favorite saint sitting there watching over us." In that moment, a seed was planted in me—maybe I'd been writing off the saints too easily. Maybe the saints aren't so distant after all. Maybe I've even known some saints in my own life?

Soon thereafter, my friend James Martin, SJ, invited me to his diaconate ordination en route to his priestly ordination. I'd never been to such a thing, so I didn't know what to expect. Early in the ordination liturgy, Jim and the other Jesuits who were being ordained deacons got down on the floor and lay prostrate as the congregation sang the Litany of the Saints, asking Sarah and Abraham, Mary and Joseph, Michael and the angels, and all holy women and men to pray for them.

To my surprise, I was very moved by the chant. As I looked around, family members and friends of those being ordained were visibly moved as well. Later, Jim asked me what I thought of the liturgy. When I shared with him how moving the Litany of the Saints was for me, he lit up. "Isn't that beautiful?" he said. "As we lie there on the ground as a sign of our humility and obedience, we're being lifted up by our loved ones and the entire communion of saints."

In the strict sense, a saint is someone who is recognized by the church as having lived a holy life, and who is now in heaven with God. But saints are not limited to those officially canonized by the church. Anyone who has lived a holy life can be called a saint. Not only do these saints provide models of how to live full, rich lives, they serve as "heavenly helpers" who bend God's ear on our behalf to answer our prayers.

Jim went on to write a best-selling memoir called *My Life with the Saints,* in which he explains that upon entering the Jesuit novitiate, he was surprised to learn that most of his fellow novices had strong devotions to one saint or another. He eventually read Thérèse of Lisieux's autobiography *The Story of a Soul* and got hooked on biographies of other saints, such as Stanislaus Kostka, Thomas More, Teresa of Ávila, and Pope John XXIII. The closer he got to the saints, the more he realized how human they really were. "Knowing this," he writes, "encouraged me to pray to them for help during particular times and for particular needs. . . . Quite by surprise, then, I went from someone embarrassed by my affection for the saints to someone who counted it as one of the joys of my life. . . . Now I find myself introducing others to favorite saints and, likewise, being introduced"

Jim is largely responsible for introducing me to St. Ignatius of Loyola. As my interest in Ignatius grew, the Jesuits I worked for invited me to go on a two-week pilgrimage to follow in the saint's footsteps through northern Spain and Rome.

I knew very little about St. Ignatius except the basics: He was born in 1491 near Azepeitia, Spain, to a noble family and grew up in a royal court. He became a soldier, and in 1521 was injured in a battle in Pamplona, Spain, when a cannonball hit and shattered his right leg. In two strokes of providence he was carried by his French foes home to Loyola Castle, where instead of dying he miraculously recovered and then went on to found the Society of Jesus. And truth be told, I always felt Ignatius's story was a little too ideal; it lacked a real-life fleshiness. I couldn't wait to see if there was more to the saint than the books conveyed, and if his life would speak to mine.

As our group of pilgrims met at the airport, it quickly became clear that we were an unlikely bunch—twenty-two women and men ranging in age from twenty-something to seventy-something. What we shared in common was that we all worked in one way or another at Jesuit institutions. The seven Jesuits leading the trip shared with us their hope that after visiting Madrid, Toledo, Loyola, Burgos, Javier, Barcelona, Montserrat, Manresa, and Rome, we not only would know Ignatius better but also would know God, ourselves, and each other more intimately. Ultimately, that's what saints do—they teach how to love God and others.

As we set out to follow in Ignatius's footsteps (ironically, by riding on an air-conditioned bus), we were asked to put ourselves in his sandals, to experience what he experienced, and to be open to the power of God in our own lives along the way. The prayer at the start of the pilgrimage was simple: "Whoever labors to penetrate the secrets of reality with a humble and steady mind is, even if unaware, being led by the hand of God, who holds all things in existence and gives them their identity."

We began our pilgrimage in Loyola, Spain, where Ignatius was born and later had his conversion experience. Seeing his family's castle immediately made us wonder why the future saint would willingly go from such privilege to poverty, from a courtly life to a life of service. The Jesuit tour guides explained that Ignatius has been called the "pilgrim saint" because his journey was anything but linear and clear-cut. For example, when he was brought home after being wounded in battle, Ignatius thought he would recover and resume his life as a soldier. Instead, as he lay restless, recovering from his injuries, he read the only books in the house—the life of Jesus and the lives of the saints. Suddenly, he found himself experiencing a peace he had never felt before, and decided to dedicate his life to Christ. Though he had no idea what dedicating himself to Christ would mean, he prayed to be healed so that he could get on with his new pilgrimage to God, and then move out from God to the world.

When he was well enough, Ignatius traveled to the famous shrine of Montserrat in northern Spain, where he laid down his sword in front of a statue of Mary and promised to serve her son as a loving pilgrim. Having exchanged his regal clothes for those of a beggar, Ignatius then began a journey to the Holy

Land, which first took him to Manresa, Spain, where he spent a year living in a cave, praying and recording his reflections about his new faith life.

He eventually arrived in Jerusalem in 1523 and walked in the footsteps of Jesus. Though his trip was cut short because of civil unrest, Ignatius vowed to continue walking in the footsteps of Jesus for the rest of his life. As part of this vow, the pilgrim saint discerned that he needed more academic training, so at the age of thirty-three he entered a grade school and studied Latin alongside twelve-year-olds. His academic journey eventually led him to the University of Paris, where he met several of the companions who would eventually be known as the first Jesuits.

In 1539, Ignatius and his companions sought papal approval for a new order they had named the Society of Jesus; the approval was granted in 1540 by Pope Paul III. Ignatius was elected the first superior general of the order and spent the next sixteen years perfecting his book *Spiritual Exercises* (a handbook for making a retreat, which he had begun in Manresa), writing *Constitutions of the Society of Jesus,* and writing letters to Jesuits all over the world. Ignatius died on July 31, 1556, was beatified in 1609, and was canonized a saint in 1622. His international legacy is carried on by the grade schools, secondary schools, colleges, universities, hospitals, charitable institutions, publishing houses, and retreat centers that bear his name.

While the entire journey through Spain and Rome was deeply moving and gave us all deeper insight into the life of

St. Ignatius, the most powerful part of the trip for me was not being in the rooms where he was born, had his conversion experience, traded his sword for the Bible, wrote his *Constitutions* and letters, or died. Instead, the most powerful moment for me was praying in the cave in Manresa, where, at the same age as I was at the time, Ignatius struggled to discern God's unique plan for him. From the first moment we saw the cave I could imagine Ignatius, a small man of five feet, panhandling in his beggar's clothing, praying, preaching the gospel, working among the poor, and writing what would eventually become the *Spiritual Exercises* that have invited so many people into a deeper relationship with God.

As our group gathered for Mass in the cave where Ignatius spent many lonely but full hours, I felt a very real connection to him. In recent centuries the cave has been preserved alongside the adjoining Santa Cova Church. Throughout the church and the cave are many signs pointing out significant things about St. Ignatius and his journey. On the wall next to where I was seated for Mass, I noticed a glass cover protecting some markings and scribbles. A sign under the glass explained that these scribbles were from the hand of Ignatius himself. Suddenly, Ignatius became incredibly real to me.

The experience of following in Ignatius's footsteps on his path to understand who he was and what God was calling him to do continues to inspire me to make similar inquiries in my own life. As the pilgrim saint, Ignatius—like Jesus and all the saints—teaches us that the walk of faith entails embracing life's questions, seeking in as many ways as we can, and being open to conversion.

Through his example and the gift of his *Spiritual Exercises,* Ignatius encourages us to be fully alive—to find God in all things, to follow our passion and purpose, to love others as God loves us, and to serve wherever the need is greatest.

PRACTICE FOR SPIRITUAL GROWTH

In his modern-day classic *All Saints: Daily Reflections on Saints, Prophets, and Witnesses for Our Time,* Robert Ellsberg writes:

As Dorothy Day, founder of the Catholic Worker movement, used to say, "Don't call me a saint. I don't want to be dismissed that easily." By putting saints on a pedestal, we imply that their example poses no personal challenge. But when this happens, the Christian imagination is immeasurably weakened. Describing the function of the saints, Karl Rahner wrote, "They are the initiators and the creative models of the holiness which happens to be right for, and is the task of, their particular age. They create a new style; they prove that a certain form of life and activity is a really genuine possibility; they show experimentally that one can be a Christian even in 'this' way; they make such a type of person believable as a Christian type." The saints are those who, in some partial way, embody—literally incarnate—the challenge of faith in their time and place. In doing so, they open a path that others might follow.

Take some time to reflect on this passage:

■ *What qualities make someone a saint?*

■ *What did Dorothy Day mean when she said, "Don't call me a saint. I don't want to be dismissed that easily"?*

■ *Is there any value in looking to the saints for direction and inspiration?*

■ *Challenge yourself to read about the lives of the saints and draw ideas and inspiration from their lives.* Butler's Lives of the Saints *or* Ellsberg's All Saints *are good resources.*

In 2007, people around the world were surprised by the revelation that Mother Teresa, the "saint of the gutters," battled with spiritual darkness, doubt, and despair for fifty years. Reports of her "dark night," as St. John of the Cross would call it, began circulating in 2003. But it wasn't until the 2007 publication of *Mother Teresa: Come Be My Light,* a collection of Mother Teresa's letters originally gathered to build the case for her canonization, that people realized the dramatic extent to which she struggled with her faith.

Mother Teresa was born in 1910 to a Catholic family in Albania and given the name Agnes Gonxha Bojaxhiu. In 1928, Agnes entered the Sisters of Loreto in Ireland and took the name Sister Mary Teresa. Soon thereafter she was sent to India to work in a girls' school in Calcutta, where she took final vows for her order and was given the title Mother. In 1946, Mother Teresa had a powerful mystical experience in which Jesus asked her to work with the poorest of the poor. She eventually left the Sisters of Loreto and founded her own order, the Missionaries of Charity, where she began ministering to the poor and dying.

From that time on, she felt only God's absence from her life. Sometimes she felt like a hypocrite, but as she explains in her letters, she didn't want to discuss her struggles publicly for fear that she would direct focus on herself and away from Jesus. She continued with her ministry to the poor and eventually became a household name, particularly when she received the Nobel Peace Prize.

In the years since her death in 1997, Blessed Teresa of Calcutta has begun a new ministry to those who doubt, experience God's absence, or disbelieve. Her own form of grappling with questions of God's existence and her pain from God's absence in her life included writing, reading, loving others, and serving those in the greatest need. In some ways, her status as a living saint made her service to the poor even more difficult. Yet, rather than despair, she became all the more committed to the mission she started when, as a young woman, she heard God's voice for the first, and the last, time.

■ *What's your reaction to the revelation that Mother Teresa experienced fifty years of spiritual darkness, doubt, and despair?*

■ *Robert Ellsberg writes, "The saints are those who, in some partial way, embody—literally incarnate—the challenge of faith in their time and place. In doing so, they open a path that others might follow." What path does Mother Teresa's life provide for people today, especially for those who struggle with faith?*

■ *Who are the "saints" in your life? What paths have these holy women and men opened up for you, and where have you gone as a result?*

■ *What kinds of saints are needed today?*

■ *Consider the quotation from Thomas Merton that began this chapter. What do you think he means when he says that being a saint means being yourself?*

■ *Are you fully alive? Are you fulfilling your purpose in life? Do you live with passion and joy? What changes would you make in your life to be more fully alive?*

■ *What lessons do you think your attitudes and way of being teach others? What legacy do you hope to leave behind?*

14 Where Am I Going, and How Do I Get There?
The Practice of Spiritual Direction

The Christian Life—and especially the contemplative life—
is a continual discovery of Christ in new and unexpected
places.

—Thomas Merton

REFLECTION

In his *The Heart of Christianity,* Marcus Borg tells a story that, roughly, goes like this: A three-year-old girl was very excited for her parents to bring her new baby brother home from the hospital. When the day finally came, the little girl asked her parents if she could be alone with her new brother in his room with the door shut. Her parents were a bit uneasy about this request, but they decided it would be okay as long as they had the baby monitor on. After letting their daughter into the baby's room, the parents closed the door and then listened to the receiver of the monitor. They heard their daughter's footsteps as she approached the baby's crib; then they heard her saying to her baby brother, "Tell me about God—I've almost forgotten."

This simple story carries a profound message: We come from God, but over time we forget, lose our focus, and wander down the wrong paths. As a result, we spend a good deal of our lives trying to (re)discover who we are and what we're supposed to do with our lives.

The entire Christian tradition is dedicated to helping people find their way as sons and daughters of God. One of the practices it has always used to accomplish this mission is spiritual direction, whereby a seeker works with a mature person of faith to develop a deep relationship with God and live spiritually. Spiritual direction is not counseling or therapy or nice chats *about* God. As the term itself suggests, it's about recognizing our true spirit and pointing it in the right direction toward love and life. Specifically, it's the process by which one Christian guides another to pay attention to God in his or her life and to respond. Spiritual direction can also be thought of as spiritual companioning between two "soul friends." The focus is always on God and the directee's experience of and response to God.

The beloved spiritual guide Henri Nouwen taught that three disciplines are particularly helpful in the spiritual direction relationship: the disciplines of the heart, of the book, and of the church. In the first, we use related practices of solitude, meditation, and prayer to listen *to* and *with* the heart. We ask,

"Who am I? Who am I meant to be? What do I fear? Where is God in my life?"

The second practice uses the discipline of *lectio divina,* or sacred reading of Scripture and spiritual writings, to hear the Word of God and meditate on its meaning in our lives (see chapter 9 for more on *lectio divina*). We ask, "Who is God? Does God care for me? What does God want me to do?"

The third discipline requires us to be in relationship with others in a faith community who worship, pray, enjoy life, and help others together. We ask, "How does God act in other people's lives? Who can I look to as a model for what the walk of faith looks like? To whom am I accountable—who keeps me honest?"

After years of searching my own heart and reading theological books, I finally realized that if I wanted to grow deeper spiritual roots, I needed to be more committed to the third discipline that Nouwen describes—that of connecting with others in the faith community.

I asked a Jesuit I've known for some time, Father Daniel Flaherty, SJ, to serve as my spiritual director. He agreed and recommended that we shape our exchanges around St. Ignatius's *Spiritual Exercises.* Used widely by Christians through the centuries, the *Exercises,* like any good spiritual direction program, guide the retreatant through a process of self-awareness of good and sinful qualities, discerning God's presence and love, following Christ through his life and passion, and committing to a life of serving the risen Christ.

When we began the process, Father Dan did what any good director would do—he put me at ease. "Listen," he said in his inimitable way, "there's nothing complicated about the spiritual life. We complicate it with teachings, dogma, doctrine, theology, but what it comes down to is this: God loves you. Do you love God? If so, are you ready to commit your life to him? Are you ready to love others, *as Jesus loves you*?"

One of the first steps in spiritual direction is learning how to be open to God and to personal change by talking with a spiritual director, getting into a rhythm of daily prayer and meditation using *lectio divina* and other techniques, and logging the experiences mentally or in a journal. What struck me the most when I began my spiritual direction, and still does today, is that a central component to the process is asking God for a particular grace and expressing what I want out of prayer and in my life. These actions of "heart speaking to heart" make prayer a real conversation with God. From this practice, all else in the spiritual life flows.

As Father Dan and I worked together for the next few months, I felt like things were going really well. I was in a solid groove of praying with the prescribed passage and journaling about various aspects of my faith each evening before bed. I was reading Scripture commentary and other spiritual and theological works. And my weekly conversations with Father Dan were consistently lively and rich.

Then, one week, Father Dan listened patiently as I described all that I'd learned about God and how a past trip to the Holy Land had helped me relate to the landscape and details I had pondered in that week's meditations. After I finished, he said, simply, "That's all well and good, but I don't hear you talking about feeling called by Jesus. What do you think Jesus wants of you at this moment, and are you willing to answer his call? Are you willing to follow him to the cross and beyond?"

He was right. Or, more accurately, he prompted me to face the truth that after months of prayer and meditation and study, I'd still been approaching God academically, at a distance. "Look," he said, "from the time I was a novice, I've been the world's best meditator. And I can talk about Scripture till the cows come home. But that's not the point. The point is to get to know Jesus."

At that moment, my prayer life and my faith moved into a more productive direction. In the following weeks and months, I studied less and practiced the exercises more. I plowed through prayer less and talked with God more. I talked about spiritual direction less and headed in a more spiritual direction in my daily life.

But just like eating right and staying in shape, spiritual exercise is a lifelong process. Thinking of my path ahead, I once asked Father Dan if he would share with me, in his eightieth year, how he practices the exercises in his daily life: "It's simple," he said. "I try to love others, *as Jesus loves us,* and check in twice a day to see if I'm living the life Christ wants me to live."

PRACTICE FOR SPIRITUAL GROWTH

Two of the primary questions in the spiritual life are "Where am I going?" and "How do I get there?" The practice of spiritual direction is a wonderful way to address these two questions. By working with a trusted spiritual mentor, we learn how to be honest with ourselves. We identify where we are in the spiritual life, and where we want to be. We learn to have eyes to see and ears to hear God at work in our lives. And we hold ourselves accountable to various disciplines such as study, prayer, solitude, reflection, journaling, and service.

▪ *Challenge yourself to find a spiritual director at your church or in your faith community.*

Saint Ignatius's *Spiritual Exercises* offer a wide range of practices for developing a healthy spiritual life. One of them is the examination of conscience, or the daily examen. The examen is a restful prayer that allows us to examine and evaluate the hours of the day in light of three central questions:

▪ *What have I done for Christ?*
▪ *What am I doing for Christ?*
▪ *What ought I do for Christ?*

The examen typically takes ten to fifteen minutes and might be done in the middle or at the end of the day (both, if possible). Joan L. Roccasalvo, CSJ, wrote an excellent version of it called *Prayer for Finding God in All Things: The Daily Examen of St. Ignatius of Loyola,* cited below. Start by committing to practice the examen one day or evening. Then challenge yourself to practice it every day for a week. Then a month. Eventually, it might become a routine part of your daily faith life.

1 Overview of the day. What is holding your attention now? What did you do and experience today? How did you feel and behave? How do you feel now as you look back over your day?

2 Gratitude. Thank God for the gift of life. What else can you thank God for today?

3 Prayer. Ask God to help you to be open and honest with yourself about who you are and how you are living your life.

4 God. Do you know your need for God? Did you spend time in prayer today? If not, what hindered you? If you did, how did your prayer go?

5 Self. What habitual attitude or attachment do you hold onto that impairs your relationship with God, yourself, and the world? Where is there too much or too little in your life? What attitude drives your life? Did you spread joy or negativity today?

6 Others. Did you thank others for their help and kindness? Were you patient, tolerant, and kind? Were you cross and judgmental?

7 Circumstances. How did you deal with today's difficulties? Did you practice the sacrament of the present moment? How did your basic faults affect today's events? Did you ask God for help today? Did you see God in your day?

8 Ecology. Did you express gratitude for the beauty of creation through your actions?

9 Sorrow for your faults. Were you aware of your shortcomings, and did you ask God for forgiveness?

10 Resolve to make a fresh start. "With thanks for my life, I resolve to live as closely to God as possible."

11 Closing prayer. "Our Father . . ."

THREE BRANCHES

He also said, "With what can we compare the kingdom of God, or what parable will we use for it? It is like a mustard seed, which, when sown upon the ground, is the smallest of all the seeds on earth; yet when it is sown it grows up and becomes the greatest of all shrubs, and puts forth large branches, so that the birds of the air can make nests in its shade."

—Mark 4:30–32

Introduction

I've never seen a mustard seed, but I have seen a radish seed, and they're pretty small and pretty remarkable. You make a row in the soil, sprinkle in seeds you can barely see, and soon enough you're plucking some big radishes out of the ground and throwing them in a salad.

If the kingdom of heaven is like a mustard seed, or a radish seed for that matter, then it's difficult to see with the naked eye. But if we look through the lens of faith, sure enough, we can see it. Then the question becomes what we have to do to nurture its growth in our lives. Using the parable of the sower and the spiritual practices covered so far, we know that we have to cultivate the soil of our lives to receive the seed and then encourage the root growth that takes place slowly and quietly below the surface. Then we wait. And we water. And we talk to other spiritual gardeners. We might even talk to the seeds as they take root. Then, one day, the sprout shoots up through the soil toward heaven and begins to "put forth branches." While the branches are strong, they still require care and need to be pruned from time to time to make sure the sun and the soil's energy maximizes the living potential.

In John's Gospel, Jesus carries the metaphor one step further and explains its meaning:

> I am the true vine, and my Father is the vinegrower. He removes every branch in me that bears no fruit. Every branch that bears fruit he prunes to make it bear more fruit. You have already been cleansed by the word that I

have spoken to you. Abide in me as I abide in you. Just as the branch cannot bear fruit by itself unless it abides in the vine, neither can you unless you abide in me. I am the vine, you are the branches. Those who abide in me and I in them bear much fruit, because apart from me you can do nothing. Whoever does not abide in me is thrown away like a branch and withers; such branches are gathered, thrown into the fire, and burned. If you abide in me, and my words abide in you, ask for whatever you wish, and it will be done for you. My Father is glorified by this, that you bear much fruit and become my disciples. As the Father has loved me, so I have loved you; abide in my love. If you keep my commandments, you will abide in my love, just as I have kept my Father's commandments and abide in his love.

Paul teaches that the "branches" of the spiritual life bear fruits of love, joy, peace, patience, kindness, generosity, faithfulness, gentleness, and self-control.

The disciplines in this final section are meant to cultivate the branches and harvest the fruit that have grown from the seeds that you've nurtured in the soil of your life. Here we explore the practices of listening to your life for your true vocation, being an active member of your communities, letting go, forgiving others as you are forgiven, celebrating the gift of life, practicing virtue and charity, and living as a disciple of Christ.

Taken together, the practices in this book are meant to help you see, plant, grow, and harvest the fruit of the seeds of faith that God sows in your life. As the parable of the mustard seed reveals, even the smallest of seeds can grow into the strongest of trees.

And they do.

Spiritual wisdom to consider to help your spiritual life bear fruit:

And this, our life, exempt from public haunt, finds tongues in trees, books in the running brooks, sermons in stones, and good in everything.
—William Shakespeare

If thy heart were right, then every creature would be a mirror of life and a book of holy doctrine. There is no creature so small and abject, but it reflects the goodness of God.
—Thomas à Kempis

15 How, Then, Shall I Live?
The Practice of Vocation

> *My question . . . was the simplest question lying in the soul of every human being, from a silly child to the wisest of the elders, the question without which life is impossible; such was the way I felt about the matter. The question is this: What will come of what I do today and tomorrow? What will come of my entire life?*
>
> *Expressed differently, the question may be: Why should I live? Why should I wish for anything or do anything? Or to put it still differently: Is there any meaning in my life that will not be destroyed by my inevitably approaching death?*
>
> —Leo Tolstoy

REFLECTION

After a parish talk I'd given called "The Spirituality of Letting Go," an attractive young woman approached me to talk. "I'm really struggling right now," she said. "I was a newscaster for several years, but had to leave a good job so my husband could take a promotion at his job. Now I've been told I'm too old to get back into the television business, and I don't know who I am anymore."

After this young woman and I talked for some time, she revealed that she never really knew who she was. She earned a degree in communications and after graduation quickly fell into a job in television. "It all happened very fast," she said. "Before I knew it I was doing whatever the producer and station said I should do. And people related to me as just another pretty face on TV. But in reality, I never felt like I was doing what I was meant to do." What she really wanted to do was teach grade school, but people, including her husband and family, discouraged her, saying she was meant for more "important" work, like television.

In his *My Job, My Self*, Al Gini explains that who we are is inextricably woven together with what we do:

> Because we spend two-thirds of our waking life on the job, work is the way we come to know the world and are known to the world. Work becomes our mark of identity, our signature on the world. To work is *to be* and not to work is *not to be*. . . .
>
> Whether we have a good job or a bad one, whether we love it or hate it, succeed in it or fail, work is at the center of our lives and influences who we are and all that we do. Where we live, how well we live, whom we see socially, what and where we consume and purchase, how we educate our children—all of these are determined by the way in which

we earn a living. Work is also one of the most significant contributing factors to one's inner life and development. Beyond mere survival, we create ourselves in our work.

It's been said that "we are what we do." Because what we do shapes our personality, sense of meaning, and interaction with the world, it only makes sense that we want to love our work.

More often than not, however, we don't love our work. Job satisfaction in this country is shockingly low, leading a majority of people to draw a line between who they are at work and who they are in "real life." All too often workers describe themselves as "robots" who mindlessly perform tasks that are completely disconnected from who they are, what they love, and what they believe they are good at. Even those in high-profile, high-paying jobs report a disconnect between who they are and what they do. Doctors I've met, for example, have said that over time, especially working in emergency rooms, they begin to feel more like mechanics than human healers. One doctor said he finally became so ashamed of his lack of human interaction with patients that he took a break from the work and then started his own small practice to "save his soul."

In my conversation with the former newscaster, she said one of her greatest struggles when she was on the nightly news was that she enjoyed being recognized and respected everywhere she went, but inside she felt like "nothing more than a talking head." When she was unable to break back into television news after having children, she said her struggle had changed. "At first I wanted nothing more than to be recognized and respected again for my job," she said. "Now I just want to know who I am and to have the courage to be who God calls me to be."

It is this latter point that is at the heart of the practice of vocation. In his *Let Your Life Speak,* Parker Palmer explains that the ancient human question "Who am I?" leads inevitably to the equally important question *"Whose* am I?" By coming to see that we come from God—indeed, that we are created in the image and likeness of God—we find "the true self within every human being that is the seed of authentic vocation." Our true self lies underneath our ego and the masks we wear on a daily basis. It is our true nature, our being in its purest form.

The practice of vocation, then, is not doing what society tells us is good and desirable. It is not an act of willing ourselves to be this kind of person or have that kind of job. The practice of vocation, a word whose root comes from the Latin for "voice," means listening at the deepest level to our true selves. Palmer puts it this way:

> Before I can tell my life what I want to do with it, I must listen to my life telling me who I am. I must listen for the truths and values at the heart of my own identity, not the standards by which I *must* live—but the standards by which I cannot help but live if I am living my own life.

It's important to state clearly that the search for self and true vocation is not solipsistic. It's not about listening to ourselves in isolation or doing whatever feels good. It is quite the opposite. The practice of vocation is the practice of listening and being accountable to God, to our loved ones, to our friends and community who help us recognize our gifts. The key is to know ourselves well enough to discern if the voices in our lives lead us toward or away from our true selves.

If we listen carefully to our inner voice and what others teach us about our true self, we can answer questions such as "What do I really love? What are my greatest gifts? What type of work best expresses who I am and what I love? What type of work environment best fits my sense of creativity and values? What is my definition of success? What kind of balance do I seek between my job and my family life? What contribution to the world do I want to make through my life and work?"

The practice of vocation is not about being a doctor instead of a garbage collector; it's about tapping into what Thomas Merton describes as the "hidden wholeness" we are born with. It's what St. Irenaeus was talking about when he said, "The greatest glory of God is the human being fully alive." It's what Jesus meant when he said, "I came that they may have life, and have it abundantly."

PRACTICE FOR SPIRITUAL GROWTH

Hanging in my house is a print with the following message attributed to Pedro Arrupe, SJ, the former superior general of the Society of Jesus:

Nothing is more practical than finding God, that is, than falling in love in a quite absolute, final way. What you are in love with, what seizes your imagination, will affect everything. It will decide what will get you out of bed in the morning, what you do with your evenings, how you spend your weekends, what you read, who you know, what breaks your heart, and what amazes you with joy and gratitude. Fall in love, stay in love, and it will decide everything.

Take a moment to reflect on Father Arrupe's message:

■ *What role does God play in your life?*
■ *Who do you believe God calls you to be? How do you know?*
■ *What do you love? What gets you out of bed in the morning and gives you life?*
■ *How do you spend your days? Your weekends?*
■ *What is your vocation now? Is it your true vocation, or is there some other vocation that you would be more ideally suited for? If so, what's preventing you from seeking it?*
■ *Are you happy? Do you have balance in your life?*
■ *Are you the same person at work and at home, or do you play roles?*
■ *How might you become more integrated?*

In her poem "The Summer Day," poet Mary Oliver asks, "Tell me, what is it you plan to do / with your one wild and precious life?"

■ *Without over-thinking, write down the thoughts and feelings Oliver's questions stir in you.*
■ *It's never too late to follow your passion! Think about what your life would look like if you followed your vocational passion and were true to yourself. What would be different? What would be the same? What steps can you take in your life right now to lead you toward your true self?*

16 See How They Love One Another
The Practice of Community

The basic human need is for at least one person who
believes and trusts in us. But that is never enough, it
doesn't stop there. Each of us needs to belong, not just to
one person but to a family, friends, a group, and a culture.

—Jean Vanier, founder of l'Arche

REFLECTION

In the parable of the Good Samaritan found in Luke's Gospel, a lawyer tests Jesus by asking, "What must I do to inherit eternal life?" Jesus responds with a question of his own, "What is written in the law?" The lawyer answers, "You shall love the Lord your God with all your heart, and with all your soul, and with all your strength, and with all your mind; and your neighbor as yourself." Though Jesus indicates that the answer is correct, the lawyer presses further, "And who is my neighbor?"

Jesus responds with a parable about a man, presumably a Jew, who was robbed, beaten, and left for dead alongside the road from Jerusalem to Jericho. In the story, a priest and a Levite see the wounded man but pass on the other side of the road out of fear of violating purity laws. Eventually, a Samaritan—who were despised by Jews—comes along and immediately treats the man's wounds and takes him to an inn, paying the innkeeper to care for the man until he is restored to health. At the end of the story, Jesus asks the lawyer which of the three men on the road was a neighbor to the injured man, to which the lawyer answers, "The one who showed him mercy." Jesus concludes by saying, "Go and do likewise."

At first blush, the moral of the story is obvious: loving your neighbor as yourself means going out of your way to show kindness, even to your enemies. But, as with all of Jesus' parables, there is more to the story than meets the eye. As James Keenan, SJ, points out in his *Commandments of Compassion,* Jesus does not pass judgment on the robbers who beat up the man, but on the priest and the Levite who don't bother to love, who choose the law over the right action. Sin in the Gospels is always about not bothering to love, no matter the excuse. Jesus is always more concerned with the heart of the person than with his or her individual acts of sin.

Community is rooted in bothering to love. Two of the strongest demands of Scripture and tradition are that we welcome the stranger and serve the common good. Christian community is a form of the communion that St. Paul spoke of when he said that through the Holy Spirit, Christians enjoy fellowship with the triune God, other baptized Christians, and the world at large. As followers of Jesus, our mission is to work with and serve everyone—women and men, rich and poor, young and old, established and disenfranchised, believers and nonbelievers, healthy and infirm, free and incarcerated, those with sight and the blind—to witness to the fact that the reign of God is at hand, here and now, and is open to everyone.

The way Christians love as community stems from how we come together as church in our worship, liturgy, sacraments, virtues, prayer, and actions. And it flows out into the world when we serve the common good by honoring all people, upholding and fighting for their rights, and loving them.

In his landmark book *Bowling Alone: The Collapse and Revival of American Community,* Harvard professor Robert Putnam explains that over the past twenty-five years Americans have become increasingly disconnected from family, friends, neighbors, and social structures. The result, he says, is not only our feeling that the country is morally and civically off track, but also that we are, quite simply, less happy.

This trend away from community connections is why the Christian tradition, rooted in Trinitarian love, can seem so countercultural. Christianity calls us to befriend God and each other, to join hands, and to work together for the mutual benefit of all. It teaches that the Trinity is pure relationship. As the central mystery of our faith, the Trinity reveals that God—simultaneously creator (Father), redeemer (Son), and sanctifier (Holy Spirit)—is a living community whose actions reveal God's inmost being *and* ongoing love for creation.

As God's relationships reveal who God is, our relationships and actions reveal who we are. The way we interact with family, friends, coworkers, children, leaders, strangers on the bus or sidewalk or elevator, and the poor shows how we regard ourselves and others. As part of God's ongoing creation, we are meant to experience oneness, wholeness, happiness, forgiveness, healing, salvation. We are meant to offer these things to others. We are meant to love.

Jesus' own friendships teach us what it means to love, heal, forgive, include, magnify, revive, and even resurrect. As a young boy already teaching in the temple, Jesus came to know his earthly family not so much as superiors but as friends. When he chose his disciples, in essence his coworkers, he treated all of them with respect and tirelessly drew out the best each had to offer. When he spent time with the marginalized and dispossessed, his friendship healed. When he taught his friends how to pray, he used the word *Abba* and made possible a new kind of intimacy with the Father.

In his most trying times, Jesus' lessons on love became most clear. When he learned that his friend Lazarus had died, Jesus wept and then journeyed to the tomb and brought him back to life. When Peter, in fear for his life, denied knowing him, Jesus forgave his friend. When Jesus was condemned to death and hung on a cross, he cried out, "Father, forgive them; for they do not know what they are doing." And when, upon being raised from the dead, he appeared to his friends only to be doubted by Thomas, Jesus lovingly said, "Put your finger here and see my hands. Reach out your hand and put it in my side. Do not doubt but believe."

In Scripture Jesus teaches that the true mark of a person of faith is how he or she shows love to others. The story of the Good Samaritan teaches that loving one another isn't always convenient; in fact, sometimes it's dangerous. Obvious examples include army chaplains and ministers who work with gangs. But even when reaching out to another poses no physical harm, it can be risky. We risk hurting another's pride, or our own. We risk rejection. We risk despair. And yet, the gospel message is clear: if our faith is to mean anything, we must risk bothering to love, *as Jesus loves us.*

Loving as Jesus loves also means practicing forgiveness. Our culture sends mixed messages about sin and forgiveness, from "Don't get mad, get even" to "Forgive and forget." But Jesus teaches a different way: To turn the other cheek. To forgive those who seek forgiveness, as well as those have not apologized or even continue to wrong us. To seek out the lost sheep and do our best to bring him or her back into the fold of love and community. To ask God to forgive others who "know not what they do."

Some have interpreted Jesus' message as harmful. It turns people into doormats, they argue. If we think about it, though, we know that true forgiveness is one of the toughest, most mature acts we humans can perform. There is nothing passive about forgiveness. Nothing. In truth, isn't it easier to hold a grudge against someone we feel has wronged us? Or to hate? Or to seek revenge? The act of forgiveness saves us from the slavery of such toxic emotions.

Forgiveness is an act of love. In ideal circumstances, the wrongdoer seeks forgiveness and we grant it after thought and even prayer. But we don't simply forget the wrong or our hurt from it. Rather, we reconcile with that person by charting a new, healthy way forward in the relationship, in light of the wrong. We grow from the experience. We "remember in a different way," to borrow a phrase from Father Robert Schreiter.

In many circumstances, however, the wrongdoer does not seek our forgiveness, so the acts of forgiveness and reconciliation are even tougher. In the Christian tradition, these are profound acts of faith. If God is the one who ultimately grants forgiveness and reconciliation, we participate in God's freeing action by granting these to others, no matter how undeserving they may be. We do this in part to free ourselves from hatred and hurt, but more important, we do this because Jesus commands it: "Do not judge, and you will not be judged; do not condemn, and you will not be condemned. Forgive, and you will be forgiven."

By caring for the good of others and practicing forgiveness, we become outward symbols of God's love. Just as the health of a tree is determined by the bloom of its branches, the health of the human community is known by the way its members love one another.

PRACTICE FOR SPIRITUAL GROWTH

As the church transitions from Lent to Easter during Holy Week, it is common in liturgical traditions to reenact Jesus' washing of the disciples' feet on Holy Thursday. Each year it strikes me how reluctant people are at first to get their feet washed by the priest or others. Having your feet washed or washing someone else's feet is uncomfortable, humbling, intimate. Yet, it is also liberating. Inevitably, once enough brave souls line up to have their feet washed and to wash the feet of another, more and more people join in. Sometimes, the process can go on for what seems an eternity!

The washing of the feet provides a powerful metaphor for what community is all about: caring for others—even strangers—and allowing ourselves to be cared for by others at an intimate level. The following reflections and practices will help you examine and strengthen your communities:

■ *Reflect on what community means to you: What communities do you presently belong to? Who are the people who comprise these communities and what do they center around? Who are the leaders? Is everyone treated equally? Are some people "more equal" than others? Do you find your various communities life-giving? Why or why not? Are there any communities you are a member of that you wish you were not? Likewise, are there any communities you wish you belonged to? What has prevented you from becoming a member?*

■ *Now, reflect on the meaning of "the common good." In what ways do your friends and communities serve the common good in your neighborhood, workplace, parish, city?*

■ *Challenge yourself to think about the true meaning of community and to assess how you might enter into community life more fully. For some, this might mean joining a book or gardening club, a parish, or Bible study group.*

■ *Set short- and long-term goals for what you hope to accomplish in your various communities. You could volunteer at a soup kitchen, literacy program, or Big Brother/Big Sister program. You could organize a group to clean the local park. Be creative in how you practice "bothering to love."*

■ *A vital practice to helping to build a healthy community is forgiveness. Take a moment to reflect on how you might better practice forgiveness and reconciliation in your own life: Whom might you forgive and reconcile with? From whom might you seek forgiveness and reconciliation? Challenge yourself to practice reconciliation with anyone where open wounds continue to cause pain in your life.*

17 How Do I Get Free? How Do I Stay Free?
The Practice of Letting Go

Therefore I tell you, do not worry about your life, what you will eat or what you will drink, or about your body, what you will wear. . . . Look at the birds of the air; they neither sow nor reap nor gather into barns, and yet your heavenly Father feeds them. Are you not of more value than they? And can any of you by worrying add a single hour to your span of life? And why do you worry about clothing? Consider the lilies of the field, how they grow; they neither toil nor spin, yet I tell you, even Solomon in all his glory was not clothed like one of these. . . . Therefore do not worry, saying, "What will we eat?" or "What will we drink?" or "What will we wear?". . . Strive first for the kingdom of God and his righteousness, and all these things will be given to you as well.

So do not worry about tomorrow, for tomorrow will bring worries of its own. Today's trouble is enough for today.

—Matthew 6:25–34

REFLECTION

After many years of ministering to people of all walks of life, Father John Cusick has distilled the spiritual quest into two questions: "How do I get free?" and "How do I stay free?" "At some point or another," he says, "people want to know how they can get free so they can get on with living more fully."

Before these questions are philosophical or theological, they're practical. We humans believe we have a right to be free—physically, emotionally, intellectually, spiritually. But how can we be free if we live in fear for our safety or are paralyzed by insecurity, addiction, or shame? If we're weighed down by our past failures or defined by what others think of us? If we're quick to judge and slow to reconcile? Or, if we're utterly determined to control every aspect of our lives?

If you're like me, you find sayings like "Let go, let God," and "Bloom where you're planted" cliché. Yet, if we stop and think about them, they're loaded with wisdom. The passage above from Matthew's Gospel helps us unpack the truth these pithy statements reveal. In it, Jesus asks his disciples to "consider the lilies of the field." If we take a moment to practice this exercise of consideration, we see that the lily does not choose the field or the quality of the soil in which it is planted. It doesn't have control over what grows around it, whether thorns that threaten to choke it out or sunflowers that eclipse its beauty. It cannot control the weather or its shape, color, and size. And yet, Jesus explains, in the eyes of God, not even Solomon in all his finery was any more lovely than that lily.

The message of this passage becomes clear: we're not in control of our lives, God is. So the simple yet complex answer to the questions "How do I get free?" and "How do I stay free?" is to let go, and let God.

More specifically, letting go is a kind of detachment—from our possessions, passions, goals, plans. In her book *Amazing Grace,* Kathleen Norris explains that while the word *detachment* has lost its positive connation and is most often used negatively to mean the opposite of a healthy engagement with the world and others, it was valued by early Christians as a virtue. To be detached meant to be free from distractions and desires that got in the way of a robust relationship with God and others. To practice detachment meant actively letting go of one's own control and desired outcomes in favor of trusting in God's love, God's plan for us, and God's timeline. The result of such detachment is freedom: to accept God's love and move out into the world with a belief that, flawed as we are, we have an important purpose.

In the Christian tradition, freedom is called "salvation," which comes from the Latin word *salvus,* meaning "safe," and is related to the word *salus,* meaning "good health." Christian salvation is both *freedom from* things like sin, suffering, and death, and *freedom for* things like union with God, happiness, and life everlasting. On the most practical level, Christians believe that God creates each of us to be whole and happy.

The defining characteristic of Christian salvation is that God is the one who frees us to be most fully alive. In John's Gospel, Jesus declares, "I came that they may have life, and have it abundantly." The Christian response, then, to the questions "How do I get free?" and "How do I stay free?" is through faith and trusting God.

The spiritual truth is that no matter how hard we try we can't save ourselves. We need God. We also need each other. The goal of Christian salvation is not merely individual freedom; it's communal freedom that allows all people to be fully alive. Jesus and the church teach that salvation and spiritual freedom come by loving God and neighbor, who teach us who we really are and allow us to share our gifts with the world.

In the spiritual classic *The Way of a Pilgrim,* an anonymous nineteenth-century Russian peasant explores how the practice of letting go and being spiritually free is interwoven with the practice of prayer. Driven by the desire to follow Christ and understand what St. Paul means when he instructs believers to "pray without ceasing," this pilgrim travels to churches, monasteries, and sacred sites all over Russia in search of holy men and women who can provide an answer. He simply cannot understand how anyone could pray constantly "when the practical necessities of life demand so much attention."

This pilgrim's quest to learn how to pray at all times may strike us today as over the top. We've come to accept that juggling the daily demands of our busy lives requires us to divide our days—even ourselves—into categories and tasks. Who we are and what we do at work are not necessarily the same as who we are and what we do at home or while out with friends, on vacation, reading a book, sitting in the pew at church. When it comes to faith, it's all we can do to make it to church on Sunday or pray once in a while. A friend of mine spoke for many when she explained, "If I don't put 'God' on my to-do list, I simply forget to pray or go to church."

What would my life be like if instead of putting God on my

to-do list, I put God at the center of my life? If I trusted God enough to give up my tight control of how I present myself to others or manipulate God and others to bend to my will? If I spent more time *being* rather than *doing,* enjoying creation, feeling loved, and helping others feel loved?

As the Russian peasant who wrote *The Way of the Pilgrim* eventually learned, the paradox of Christian freedom is that the more we let go and trust God, the freer and happier we become. With the help of a spiritual guide and the writings of the church fathers, the pilgrim learns the Jesus Prayer (or the Prayer of the Heart) and finds himself deeply enlightened by repeating it over and over: "Lord Jesus Christ, have mercy on me."

The desert fathers taught that this simple prayer is a summary of the gospel message, and that ceaseless recitation of it leads to a union with God so powerful that the pray-er joins his or her will with God's and comes to see the world through God's eyes.

The Jesus Prayer is not a magic formula, but a way of being. By paying attention to what is in his heart and asking for God's mercy, the pilgrim learns to make each moment of each day a prayer in response to God's love and forgiveness. By "praying ceaselessly" with his very life, he experiences "great joy" and spends the rest of his life teaching others how to be free by "letting go, letting God."

PRACTICE FOR SPIRITUAL GROWTH

As *The Way of the Pilgrim* reveals, the practice of "letting go, letting God" is intimately tied to the practice of prayer. Make time in your day or evening to follow the ancient directives for praying the Jesus Prayer listed below:

1 Sit or stand in a dimly lit and quiet place.
2 Re-collect yourself.
3 With the help of your imagination, find the place of the heart and stay there with attention.
4 Lead the mind from the head into the heart and say, "Lord Jesus Christ, have mercy on me," quietly out loud or mentally, whichever is more convenient; say the prayer slowly and reverently.
5 As much as possible, guard the attention of your mind and do not allow any thoughts to enter in.
6 Be patient and peaceful.
7 When you are finished, record any thoughts and feelings you experienced as you prayed.

■ *Consider the freedom and purpose you feel or would like to feel in your life: What does it mean to be free? Do you believe that God loves you and has a special purpose for you? If so, what is your purpose? What holds you back from living your purpose? How can you overcome these obstacles to personal and spiritual freedom? How might your life be a living testimony to the power of spiritual freedom?*

Other practices that typically accompany the Jesus Prayer speak to living a simpler, more focused lifestyle:

■ *Be moderate in food, drink, and sleep.*
■ *Learn to love silence.*
■ *Read the Scriptures and the writings of the church fathers about prayer.*
■ *As much as possible, avoid distracting occupations.*

18 Happy Are They
The Practice of Celebration

You are the salt of the earth. . . .
You are the light of the world.
 —Matthew 5:13–14

REFLECTION

On my office wall is a bronze plaque engraved with the words: "Bidden or not bidden, God is present." The plaque holds sentimental value because it was given to me by a close friend. It also serves as a daily reminder that, whether I recognize it or not, God is always with me. The psychologist Carl Jung came across this phrase in its original Latin form, *"Vocatus atque non vocatus deus aderit,"* as a young student researching Erasmus's writings. He liked it so much that he had it carved over the front door of his house in Zurich to remind those entering that "awe of the LORD is the beginning of wisdom." Erasmus himself had the phrase carved on his tombstone.

Practicing the spiritual disciplines in this book is a way of engraving these words on our hearts. Whether you ask for it or not, God is present. God is in the details; we just have to know where to look and how to see. God calls and it's up to us to respond. God is the Good Shepherd who leaves the flock to retrieve the one lost sheep. God is the "hound of heaven," to quote the poet Francis Thompson, who seeks us even when we try to flee.

"OK," said one young woman during a parish discussion, "let's say I buy it. Let's say I believe that God is in all things, and that God wants a personal relationship with me. Now what? What does it mean to believe in God?"

The group fell silent. Then, a man in his fifties who hasn't had an easy life, said, "You celebrate. You walk around like you know you're loved, no matter what. You help people. And you smile."

It sounds simple, doesn't it? But just try it, even for a week. Try to begin and end your day in gratitude. Try to remember that you are loved, that you are the light of the world. Try to help people, even those you simply can't stand. And smile. Research tells us that just by smiling, you conjure feelings of happiness. Go ahead, try it—just smile. Even if you don't feel all that different, maybe someone just saw you smile and you made them feel good!

Saint Irenaeus's line, "The greatest glory of God is the human being fully alive," is an incredible piece of spiritual wisdom. Think about it: By being happy, we make God happy. And who doesn't want to be happy? The disciples certainly wanted to experience joy and happiness. The crowds who looked to Jesus for answers did, too. So what did Jesus teach about happiness? Matthew tells us, "When Jesus saw the crowds, he went up to the mountain; and after he sat down, his disciples came to him. Then he began to speak, and he taught them, saying:

How happy are the poor in spirit;
  theirs is the kingdom of heaven.
Happy the gentle:
  they shall have the earth for their heritage.
Happy those who mourn:
  they shall be comforted.
Happy those who hunger and thirst for what is right:
  they shall be satisfied.
Happy the merciful:
  they shall have mercy shown them.
Happy the pure in heart:
  they shall see God.
Happy the peacemakers:
  they shall be called sons of God.
Happy those who are persecuted in the cause of right:
  theirs is the kingdom of heaven.

These sayings of Jesus are called the Beatitudes, a word that stems from the Latin *beatitudo,* meaning "happiness." But they don't refer to just any happiness. Whenever Jesus speaks from the "mountain," we need to pay careful attention because he's helping us understand all that his actions are conveying. In this case, the mountain is more like a hill and is thought to be symbolic of Mount Sinai, where Moses received the Ten Commandments. So, this Sermon on the Mount is akin to commandments about living a happy, blessed, and complete life.

Jesus is not preaching about any old happiness, however; he's talking about a deep, soulful joy that is at once satisfying in the moment and a foretaste of perfect union with God in the hereafter. The Beatitudes offer practices that connect us with God and give us happiness beyond riches, fame, or power. Augustine wrote, "Our hearts are restless, O Lord, till they rest in you." The Beatitudes teach us how to rest in God and find peace, comfort, and fulfillment. Let's take a closer look.

The poor in spirit top the list of those who are promised the kingdom of heaven—that is, happiness here and now, and in life ever after. This Beatitude certainly includes the poorest of the materially poor, but it also includes those who are humble enough to admit their need of God. Humility and awe go together and are the foundation of a healthy spiritual life. A Franciscan motto that flows from the life of St. Francis of Assisi sums it up well: "The joy of poverty is to have nothing but God."

The second Beatitude most commonly refers to the meek, who shall inherit the earth. Being meek sounds like a negative trait, especially in our competitive world. But meekness doesn't mean being a doormat; it means being gentle, slow to anger, balanced, willing to accept God into your life.

The third Beatitude offers comfort to those who mourn, which includes those who have lost a loved one and those who are ill, disabled, suffering, hungry, or without hope. Mourning puts us in solidarity with others and with Christ, who suffered for us and now suffers with us. The highly respected spiritual writer and activist William Sloan Coffin once said in an NPR interview about his son's death in an auto accident, "People often ask me if I still believe in God. I tell them I do, because I believe that God was the first on the scene and the first to weep when my son died in that car."

The fourth Beatitude uses the powerful metaphor of hunger and thirst to emphasize the importance of doing what is right. In Jesus' time many people were hungry and thirsty and sought to be fed. For them, and for all, Jesus taught that nothing can feed the human person more than doing what is right. And doing what is right includes feeding and clothing and providing shelter to people who would otherwise go without. It also means fighting for the rights of others and helping those in need.

The fifth Beatitude is as simple as it is complex: to receive God's mercy, we ourselves have to show mercy. We have to forgive others for their trespasses to be forgiven for ours. While justice is a key component to building the kingdom on Earth, Jesus teaches us that justice without mercy is not God's way with us. Mercy is the distinctive and essential characteristic of Christianity: God's mercy forgives us of our sins. In turn, our mercy and charity toward others—especially the poor—heals and welcomes them into the human community while pointing to God's infinite love and mercy.

The sixth Beatitude sounds pious—happy are the pure in heart. But purity of heart is a practical, life-giving state of being. While Jesus cares deeply about our outward acts, he cares even more about what's in our hearts. To love God with our whole hearts, minds, and souls means to focus our entire being on God. Just as a baby's breathing and heart rate moves in sync with it's mother's, so our hearts move in sync with God's through prayer and spiritual practices.

The seventh Beatitude is a call to action—happy are they who make peace. Note that Jesus is not talking about those who are peaceful; the second Beatitude already covers that. This Beatitude says that the happiest people are those who are instruments of God's love and peace, as St. Francis expressed so well in his prayer.

The eighth and final Beatitude is a tough one. Jesus made no secret that his followers would be persecuted. And they were. In many ways, they still are today, even subtly, whenever the mainstream culture scoffs at believers. The great social justice champion Rev. Daniel Berrigan, SJ, has said, "If you want to be a Christian, you better look good on wood." Being a Christian means accepting suffering as part of life—carrying our crosses, and helping others carry theirs. For in the end, we believe, we will be raised into heaven and made whole.

The Beatitudes are tough stuff. They're paradoxical and go against the grain of everyday thinking. Yet, in very few words, they synthesize the essence of Christian faith—if you want to be happy, you have to be poor in spirit, you have to name your losses and mourn them, be humble, hunger for justice, show mercy, be pure in heart, build peace, and even face persecution for living your faith in God. Each of these tasks is the work of a lifetime. But along the way, if we do our best to live them, we're able to celebrate the gift of life. We can walk around with the knowledge that we are loved, no matter what. And we can let that love spill over into the lives of those around us.

The Beatitudes answer the question "What does faith look like?" with one word: happiness. To be a Christian is to be happy and to spread joy and justice. To live the good news that life has purpose and death is not the end. To enjoy the company of others and, together, to do good in the world. To laugh often and not take life too seriously. In the light of faith, happy are we . . .

PRACTICE FOR SPIRITUAL GROWTH

Write the Beatitudes on a piece of paper and spend time reflecting on each of them:

- *What does it mean to be poor in spirit? How could you live more simply? More humbly? More in tune with God? More grateful for what you have? More helpful to those who have little or nothing?*
- *What feelings arise when you think of being meek? If negative feelings arise, why? How can you think about meekness in a positive light? How might you better practice being gentle? Being slow to anger? Putting others before yourself?*
- *Why do we think we can go through life without pain or suffering? M. Scott Peck writes in his* The Road Less Traveled, *"Life is difficult." Do you accept this statement?*

What does it mean to mourn or lament? In times of pain and suffering, to whom do you turn? Do you turn to God? Do you get angry with God? Do you feel like it's wrong to ask God for help when at other times you might barely acknowledge God at all? How can suffering and mourning lead to insight and deeper faith?

■ *To hunger and thirst for what is right, for justice, means loving God and loving others as Jesus loves us. How do you express your love for God? For others? How can you do more to bring justice to those around you?*

■ *To show mercy and charity is the heart of Christianity. Do you experience God's love and forgiveness? If not, why not? Focus your spiritual practices on entering more deeply into the knowledge that you are a "loved sinner." How do you treat others? Are you judgmental? How might you show more compassion, mercy, forgiveness, and charity in your daily life?*

■ *What is a "pure" lifestyle? The goal of purity of heart is to see God more clearly, especially in the homeless, the sick, the imprisoned, the suffering. We must also realize that, just as God heals those in need, we can be healed of our afflictions and heal others of theirs. Purity of heart means being patient, loving, honest, faithful, generous, ethical. How might you use the spiritual exercises to develop a pure heart?*

■ *What is peace? In what ways are you an instrument of peace? If we are made in God's image and likeness, how can we be instruments of God's peace? Where do you experience strife in your family? In your work? In your community? What steps can you take to build peace and harmony in these places?*

▧ *What is the hardest part of being a Christian today? What makes you uncomfortable about living your faith? Can you think of examples of how you've stood up for what's right because of your faith? What were the results? What about times when you failed to act on your faith? How might you live your faith more boldly?*

If it helps, tape your list of the Beatitudes to your mirror as a daily reminder of the spiritual practices that lead to a deep, joyful faith. Note how you grow over the days, weeks, and months.

19 Moral Wisdom
The Practice of Virtue

> *This is my commandment, that you love one another as I have loved you.*
>
> —John 15:12

"Nobody ever taught me the difference between right and wrong, good and bad," an inmate told a friend of mine who volunteers as a prison minister. "And even though I probably knew the difference, it didn't matter because nobody ever made me feel like *I* was good."

The moral life is about *doing* good. But more important, it is about *being* good. In other words, who we are and what we believe determines how we act. Therefore, a healthy character and fully developed conscience naturally lead to actions that are right and good.

Throughout history, certain virtues, or qualities of character, have been considered essential to living a moral life. The classical Greek philosophers, most especially Aristotle, considered the foremost virtues to be prudence, justice, fortitude, and temperance. Later, the Romans used these "cardinal virtues" (from the Latin *cardo,* which means "hinge") to develop the *Via Romana,* or "Roman Way" of living, which they applied across their vast empire. Early Christian theologians, such as Gregory the Great and Augustine, also adopted these virtues as the "hinges" on which all other virtues in the Christian life turn.

Prudence, or practical wisdom, is hailed as the most important of the cardinal virtues because it enables us to discern the course of action most in keeping with the moral life. Justice enables us to champion what is fair for every person. Fortitude enables us to have the courage to do the right thing, no matter the cost. And temperance enables us to maintain a correct balance in life.

Relying on the works of Aristotle and Augustine, Thomas Aquinas developed the concept of virtue within the Catholic Christian tradition by making an important clarification about the role of the intellect in the moral life. In his *Summa Theologiae,* Aquinas refers to a virtue as a "habit," or a way of being in which a person does what is morally right according to the proper intention. For Aquinas, what makes an act morally right is not only the act itself, but also the motivation behind the act. Virtuous people practice prudence by both understanding what the moral life entails and willingly applying that knowledge to concrete circumstances in daily life. They practice temperance by consciously exercising self-control in the face of passions or temptations that might deter them from the right action. They practice justice by ensuring that each person gets his or her due. And they practice fortitude by being courageous in their resolve to do what is morally good, no matter the consequences.

The very essence of Christianity is moral living—knowing what is right and wrong, and doing what is right. But it is not enough to "do good and avoid evil." The goal of the Christian life is to follow Christ, to share in his life and conform ourselves to his way by loving all of creation. While the cardinal virtues are key practices that help Christians, and all people, live morally upright lives, Jesus calls us to go further: Jesus calls us to love.

From his earliest days, Jesus loved his earthly parents, Mary and Joseph. As he grew to understand that he was also the Son of God, he addressed his divine Father lovingly as Abba, or "Papa," and shared that divine love with the world, especially with sinners, outcasts, the sick, and the poor. Love was and is Jesus' moral code. In love, Jesus taught, healed, and performed miracles to reveal God's love for the world that God had created and called "good" from the very beginning of time. In love, Jesus subjected himself to rejection, emotional and physical pain and suffering, and death at the hands of humans who did not understand, who coveted power, who feared. In love, Jesus was raised from the dead by his Father and sent his Spirit to imbue the universe with love and to make a "new creation" of anyone who chooses to live in Christ and act on Christ's behalf.

As if to represent us all, a scribe in Mark's Gospel asks Jesus which commandment, which practice, is the most important. Referring to words from Deuteronomy, Jesus responds, "Hear, O Israel: the Lord our God, the Lord is one; you shall love the

Lord your God with all your heart, and with all your soul, and with all your mind, and with all your strength." Then Jesus adds a second commandment: "You shall love your neighbor as yourself." In John's account of the Last Supper, Jesus goes one step further by instructing his disciples:

> As the Father has loved me, so I have loved you; abide in my love. If you keep my commandments, you will abide in my love, just as I have kept my Father's commandments and abide in his love. I have said these things to you so that my joy may be in you, and that your joy may be complete.
>
> This is my commandment, that you love one another *as I have loved you.*

From these passages we see the virtues that the Christian tradition calls the theological virtues of *faith, hope,* and *love.* Unlike other virtues, the theological virtues are not acquired by personal effort but are received as gifts from God. Yet, like all virtues, they must be practiced if they are to be made real.

The practice of *faith* means entering into an intimate relationship with God, who creates us, invites us into friendship, and loves us all the days of our lives. The practice of *hope* means holding the belief that union with God is possible here on Earth and, more perfectly, in the life to come. The practice of *love* or, more accurately, *charity,* is the soil from which all other virtues grow and develop.

As is made clear over and over in the Gospels, charity is the highest form of the Christian love that originates from and is directed toward the triune God, who is love. The practice of love means treating everyone as neighbors by caring for them not only as we ourselves wish to be cared for, but as God cares for us. In the Christian life, the virtues of faith, hope, and love are all essential, but "the greatest of these is love." To love God is to love ourselves and our neighbors, and vice versa. To love God is to know that we are good and that, as a result, we are capable of doing good.

It may sound scandalous, but the message of the Gospels is that Jesus cares more about *who we are* than about *what we do.* He cares more about the content of our hearts than the individual actions of our hands. He calls all of us to conversion and, like the good shepherd, leaves ninety-nine in the field to find his one lost sheep. He forgives all who repent and conform their lives to his.

The practice of virtue, then, is the practice of love. From love—love of God, love of self, and love of neighbor—all else in the moral life flows. The danger in writing about love is that we sap it of its energy by analyzing and translating it into lists and rules for living a moral life. We worry more about avoiding sin and completing checklists than living a good life rooted in God's love.

Lists and rules are helpful, as any parent or teacher knows, but they are meaningless if we treat them as ends in themselves. As Socrates said, to be virtuous we need to surround ourselves with people who are virtuous. That is, we need to imitate them and reflect on what it looks and feels like to love, to have faith, to hope, and to practice prudence, justice, temperance, and fortitude. Then we need to give witness so that our lives tell the story of God's love affair with the world.

So let us end where we began—with the story of the inmate and the prison minister. My friend visited this prisoner for several years. Some days they sat in silence, but most days the man told my friend all the terrible things he'd done and how little he thought of himself. Each visit, my friend made sure she was entirely present to this man. She made eye contact with him, asked him questions, and offered her thoughts on what he'd said. She always finished her visits by saying, "I look forward to our next visit." Then, one day, the man broke down crying and said, "Thank you."

"For what?" my friend asked.

"For showing me what it feels like to be loved, to feel like I'm good. And for inspiring me to do something good with my life."

PRACTICE FOR SPIRITUAL GROWTH

Locate stories in Scripture in which Jesus heals, forgives, performs a miracle, or teaches.

- *What do you notice about these stories?*
- *What does Jesus focus on—the work of human hands, or the content of the human heart?*
- *How might you live his admonition, "Now go and do likewise," in your daily life?*
- *What are the greatest challenges to living a moral life?*
- *How might you incorporate the cardinal and theological virtues into your daily life?*

20 When Did We See You Hungry?
The Practice of Mercy

Love never ends. But as for prophecies, they will come to an end; as for tongues, they will cease; as for knowledge, it will come to an end. For we know only in part, and we prophesy only in part; but when the complete comes, the partial will come to an end. When I was a child, I spoke like a child, I thought like a child, I reasoned like a child; when I became an adult, I put an end to childish ways. For now we see in a mirror, dimly, but then we will see face to face. Now I know only in part; then I will know fully, even as I have been fully known. And now faith, hope, and love abide, these three; and the greatest of these is love.
—1 Corinthians 13:8–13

REFLECTION

The man sitting next to me on the airplane was looking over my shoulder to see what I was reading. When he realized that it was an article on a young man who was leading his church on a mission to fight homelessness and hunger in his community, he felt compelled to share.

"Homelessness is a terrible thing," he began.

"Absolutely," I agreed, trying to keep my focus on the page before me.

"It's a downright sin to allow people to be homeless in our communities," he said with great conviction. Before I knew it, we were talking about how our shared Christian faith requires us to share love and mercy with those in need. He went on to tell me a story that has stayed with me.

"I belong to a huge suburban church that has all the bells and whistles," he said. "But one day I realized that for all our high-energy Sunday sermons, we weren't doing much more than feeling good about ourselves for going to church. So, I challenged the pastor to address some need in the community."

"After some time," the man continued, "the pastor delivered a sermon about the rampant problem of homelessness in our area and our call to address this issue as disciples of Christ. When he was finished, he called all of us in attendance to walk up to the front of the church and donate our shoes. To my amazement, nearly every single person in that congregation donated his or her shoes and returned to their pews in their socks and bare feet. You never saw such a pile of shoes!"

In Matthew's final judgment scene, Jesus separates the sheep (those who are saved) from the goats (those who aren't saved) based on the acts of mercy they showed him:

> The king will say to those at his right hand, "Come, you that are blessed by my Father, inherit the kingdom prepared for you from the foundation of the world; for I was hungry and you gave me food, I was thirsty and you gave me something to drink, I was a stranger and you welcomed me, I was naked and you gave me clothing, I was sick and you took care of me, I was in prison and you visited me."

But the righteous are confused and ask:

> "Lord, when was it that we saw you hungry and gave you food, or thirsty and gave you something to drink? And when was it that we saw you a stranger and welcomed you, or naked and gave you clothing? And when was it that we saw you sick or in prison and visited you?"

Jesus explains:

> "Truly I tell you, just as you did it to one of the least of these who are members of my family, you did it to me."

Mercy is the defining characteristic of Christianity, but this is not just any mercy; it's mercy without reward.

For a good part of Christian moral history, people were taught to show mercy to the stranger because that person might just be Jesus in disguise. It's a powerful image, to look deeply into others, especially those in need, to see the face of Christ. And it also provides a strong motivation to be good and ethical to others on the chance that you might hit the jackpot and be rewarded with eternal salvation.

But, as the parable of the last judgment teaches, such an application of mercy is not enough. We are called to show mercy to those in need precisely because they are people in need. Rather than gambling that the one being helped might really be Christ, we are called to show mercy and charity to others *as Christ shows mercy to us*. By valuing each person as a child of God, Jesus teaches, we actually serve God.

Mercy is the richest form of love, and without it there can be no justice or peace. R.C. Lewontin makes the point this way:

According to a Haggadic legend, when God decided to create the world he said to Justice, "Go and rule the earth which I am about to create." But it did not work. God tried seven times to create a world ruled by Justice, but they were all failures and had to be destroyed. Finally, on the eighth try, God called in Mercy and said, "Go, and together with Justice, rule the world that I am about to create, because a world ruled only by Justice cannot exist." This time, apparently, it worked, more or less.

Yet, the nature of mercy, and this is very surprising to some, is that it will only be shown to those who are themselves merciful.

James teaches, "Judgment will be without mercy to anyone who has shown no mercy; mercy triumphs over judgment."

The lesson here is not to show mercy to others for fear of eternal damnation. The lesson is to practice mercy because that is what everyone from Moses to Jesus has done as the definitive response to God's love and mercy.

A final story: An elderly nun who'd devoted her life to serving the poor gave a talk at an urban community center about God's call to love and serve others, especially those in the greatest need. At the end of the talk, a middle-aged man in the back of the room raised his hand. When the nun called on him, he said, "That's all well and good, Sister, but let me ask you something: With all the crime, hatred, war, illness, disease, and suffering in the world, why hasn't *God* done anything to help those in need?!"

Without hesitating, the nun looked into the man's eyes and said, "God has done something, my friend—he put you here." Then, looking at each person in the room, she said, "God put you on this earth to be his hands and his body—to *do* something. The rest is up to you."

PRACTICE FOR SPIRITUAL GROWTH

The life of faith pivots around practicing mercy. To help believers understand what practicing mercy entails, the Christian tradition denotes two categories of mercy—the corporal and the spiritual. As you read the list of actions associated with each category of mercy, ask yourself how you are already practicing mercy in your life, and how you can better practice mercy in your life.

The seven corporal works of mercy include:

- *Feeding the hungry*
- *Giving drink to the thirsty*
- *Sheltering the homeless*
- *Clothing the naked*
- *Visiting the sick*
- *Visiting the imprisoned*
- *Burying the dead*

These practices are paired with the spiritual works of mercy, which include:

- *Giving good counsel*
- *Teaching others*
- *Admonishing sinners*
- *Consoling the afflicted*
- *Pardoning offenses and injuries*
- *Bearing offenses patiently*
- *Praying for the living and the dead*

Individually or with your spouse or a trusted friend, choose one or two acts of mercy that you'd like to practice more regularly this year. Try to stay dedicated to your plan; if applicable, ask others to hold you accountable.

The Prayer of St. Francis has been called a summary of Christianity that one could live by. In addition to practicing the corporal and spiritual works of mercy, meditate on the Prayer of St. Francis. Dedicate one month to living out each line in your daily life. Over time, each practice of the prayer will become a part of you and your manner of being.

Lord, make me an instrument of your peace.
Where there is hatred let me sow love,
Where there is injury let me sow pardon,
Where there is doubt, faith,
Where there is despair, hope,
Where there is darkness, light,
And where there is sadness, joy.

O Divine Master,
Grant that I may not seek so much to be consoled as to console,
To be understood as to understand,
To be loved as to love.

For it is in giving that we receive,
It is in forgiving that we are forgiven,
And it is in dying that we are born to eternal life.
Amen.

21 **Following Christ**
The Practice of Discipleship

Thy Kingdom come. Thy will be done,
on earth as it is in heaven.
                    —From the Lord's Prayer

REFLECTION

A young student once asked Frank Sheed for advice on how to be a good Christian. "Get to know Jesus," replied the great publisher and Christian apologist. "I mean, really get to know *him,* not just *about* him, and you'll know the essence of your faith and how to live it through your life."

These words ran through my mind as I talked with my friend Patrick McGrath, SJ, about why he became a priest. "One night, as two Jesuit friends of mine and I were talking about the White Sox and solving the world's problems over a beer," he recalled, "I sort of tuned out of the conversation. There was a lot of noise in the bar, and as I got lost in it, I started to notice this one word that kept jumping out of what one of them was saying, and that word was *Jesus*."

Pat's initial reaction was embarrassment at talking about God in a bar. "But then my second reaction," he said, "was to be intrigued by the fact that my friend speaks so comfortably of Jesus. More than that, as St. Paul tells us, there are times when we don't know how to pray, and the Spirit sort of prays for us. In that bar that night, I experienced a deep prayer coming out of me, which was simply, 'I want that. I want what he's got— that sense of comfort and connection with Jesus.' I wanted to be a disciple of Christ."

Marcus Borg explores the meaning of being disciples of Christ in *The Heart of Christianity*. He explains that while we know Jesus' commandment to love the Lord God with all our hearts and minds, we wonder: what does it really mean to love God? "In a word," writes Borg, "it means 'practice.'" It means loving God and what God loves. It means being a committed disciple.

The words *discipleship* and *discipline* are one and the same. To make the conscious decision to follow Christ is to make the decision to live a disciplined life in the Spirit. To look through the eyes of faith and recognize God's grace and presence all around us. To listen with the ears of love to the needs of the world. To reach out with the hands of justice and mercy to serve wherever the needs are greatest.

The goal of the spiritual disciplines, then, is to help us, "through faith and grace, become like Christ by practicing the types of activities he engaged in, by arranging our whole lives around the activities he himself practiced in order to remain constantly at home in the fellowship of his father."

By following Jesus and loving as he loves, we conform our minds, hearts, and souls to his. Inward disciplines such as doubt, seeking, presence, solitude, meditation, prayer, study, vocation, and letting go help us form a relationship to the living God that transforms *who we are*.

Outward and communal disciplines such as friendship, spiritual direction, community, celebration, virtue, mercy, and service help us form a relationship with God that transforms *what we do* and *how we live*.

Together, these inward and outward practices enable us to grow the seeds of faith that God, through grace and love, plants in the soil of our lives. The point is not to practice various disciplines from time to time, but to allow them to transform us into real disciples who really believe the Good News, and who show others what the Good News looks and feels and sounds like.

No matter how attractive discipleship may seem, we know that responding to Christ's call to service is never easy. We're busy, we have our own needs to worry about, we get distracted. Christ never promised us that service would be easy, and we wouldn't want it to be. The Lutheran theologian Dietrich Bonhoeffer explains in his book *The Cost of Discipleship* that the greatest enemy of true faith is "cheap grace"; that is, the kind of grace that showers blessings without asking questions or requiring action. This is the kind of grace that means justification of sin without justification of the sinner, baptism without church discipline, communion without confession, absolution without contrition, discipleship without the cross. Cheap grace, says Bonhoeffer, is grace without Jesus Christ, living and incarnate.

If, as the book of Genesis teaches, we were created in God's image and likeness, then we have the awesome obligation to love and serve each other as God's sons and daughters. Quite simply, there's nothing cheap or easy about loving and serving others. We are creating God's kingdom on earth, which is bound to be hard work. It's what we mean when we pray, "Thy kingdom come. Thy will be done, on earth as it is in heaven."

But the reward of discipleship is great. When we become disciples of Christ, the self we have created dies, and we find instead the self that exists as a living, breathing image of the divine. We let go of the possessions that weigh us down and we become free to live more fully. We find our truest selves and, in turn, we help others find theirs in everyday life and in extraordinary ways.

Through the inward, outward, and communal disciplines, we become disciples by loving God and what God loves. As disciples, we make God's kingdom, in which dignity and love, community and compassion, mercy and justice reign, a reality for *everyone*. In the end, as the prophet Micah makes clear, what God requires of us is "to do justice, and to love kindness, and to walk humbly with your God."

PRACTICE FOR SPIRITUAL GROWTH

G.K. Chesterton wrote: "Christianity has not so much been tried and found wanting, as it has been found difficult and therefore left untried." Peace activist John Dear, SJ, offers a powerful description of what makes Christian discipleship so challenging:

Following Jesus today in a land of nuclear weapons, rampant racism, and widespread economic injustice means actively going against our culture of violence. As the culture promotes violence, we promote Jesus' nonviolence. As the culture calls for war, we call for Jesus' peace. As the culture supports racism, sexism, and classism, we demand Jesus' vision of equality, community, and reconciliation. As the culture summons us to be successful, to make money, to have a career, to get to the top, and to be number one, we race in the opposite direction and go with Jesus into voluntary poverty, powerlessness, humility, suffering, and death.

Discipleship to Jesus, according to the gospel, requires that we love our enemies, demand justice for the poor, seek liberation for the oppressed, visit the sick and the imprisoned, topple the idols of death, resist militarism, reject consumerism, dismantle racism, create community, beat swords into plowshares, and worship the God of peace. If we try to engage in these social practices, we will feel the sting of discipleship and the gospel will come alive.

Service is lived expression of faith. Service can be expressed in small acts of kindness and profound acts of social justice.

- *Reread Father Dear's passage and underline the disciplines of discipleship that you find most difficult.*
- *Challenge yourself to practice these disciplines in big and small ways in your daily life.*
- *What can you do to practice justice, mercy, and kindness more overtly in your life?*
- *What do you feel are your God-given gifts? What do others say are your greatest gifts?*
- *How might you use your gifts to serve others? What do you think God is calling you to do with your life?*
- *What have you never done to serve others that you've always wanted to do?*
- *Sign up to volunteer in your community.*
- *Learn about your local politicians—what initiatives are they involved in? What should they be doing? How can you get involved?*

Above all, I thank my wife, Liz, and our three children—Tyler, Caitlin, and Colin—for teaching me the meaning of love and community. Their support and understanding as I researched and wrote this book made all the difference.

To my parents, seasoned writers and editors themselves, for passing on their faith and taking the time to read and comment on this book. And to the other members of my family whose example and encouragement mean the world to me: Jill, Trevor, and Emily Langford; Josh, Cathy, and Sophia Langford; Erin Collier; Lindy, Paul, and Hannah Hartman. Special thanks to my in-laws, Bill and Mary Collier, for watching their grandchildren and helping around the house so Liz could finish her dissertation and I could complete this project, both of which were completed at the same time.

I'm deeply grateful to my editor, Lil Copan, for inviting me to write this book in the first place and for walking with me along the winding path that led to its completion. Besides practicing patience, Lil practiced the craft of editing at a level seldom seen in publishing anymore. I cherish her editorial wisdom, as I do her friendship.

I'm also grateful to many others at Paraclete Press who make it their mission to publish timely and timeless books on the faith life; specifically, Lillian Miao, CJ, Pamela Jordan, Jon Sweeney, Sr. Mercy Minor, CJ, Jennifer Lynch, Karen Minster, and Robert Edmonson, CJ, who carefully edited and shepherded this book through the production process.

I owe a debt of gratitude to Pat McGrath, sj, and John Jones for their friendship and helpful feedback on the text. Many other friends deserve recognition, particularly, Rev. John Cusick, G.R. Kearney, Bill and Beth Cadigan, Grant Gallicho, Les and Linda Seitzinger, Andy and Lari Cavallari, Michelle and Karl Clifton-Soderstrom, Dave Collins, sj, Andy and Anj Pauline, Joe Downey, sj, Colleen and Brad Kave, Chris Devron, sj, Matthew Lynch, Catherine Cassidy, and Laura Lehmann.

Finally, to the Jesuits and my coworkers at the Chicago Province of the Society of Jesus: namely, Ed Schmidt, sj; Rick Millbourn, sj; Daniel Flaherty, sj; Jim Gschwend, sj; Pat Fairbanks, sj; Bob Flack, sj; Tim Freeman; Eileen Fitzpatrick; Jeff Smart; George Sullivan; Kathy Raccuglia; Kay Smolinski; and Eileen Meehan.

Introduction

v   *Every moment*   Thomas Merton, *New Seeds of Contemplation* (Boston: Shambhala, 2003), 16.

vi   *God planted*   Genesis 2:8–3:8.

viii *That same day*   Matthew 13:1–9.

ix   *The reason*   Matthew 13:10–13.

     In his explanation   Matthew 13:18–23.

x   *The goal*   I owe a debt of gratitude to Megan McKenna, for the insights in her book *Parables: The Arrows of God* (Maryknoll, NY: Orbis Books, 1994), 31–57.

ONE SEEDS

1 Who Am I? The Practice of *Spirit*-uality

5   *Many spiritual traditions*   Wayne Muller, *How, Then, Shall We Live? Four Simple Questions That Reveal the Beauty and Meaning of Our Lives* (New York: Bantam Books, 1996), 3.

7   *Spirituality is not*   Ronald Rolheiser, *The Holy Longing: The Search for a Christian Spirituality* (New York: Doubleday, 1999), 6–7.

2 Why Believe? The Practice of Doubt

12   *Doubt*   Jennifer Michael Hecht, *Doubt: A History: The Great Doubters and Their Legacy of Innovation, from Socrates and Jesus to Thomas Jefferson and Emily Dickinson* (New York: HarperCollins, 2006), xxi.

15   *Going*   Matthew 26:38–39.

      My God   Matthew 27:46.

16 *Unless I See* John 20:24–25.

Jesus came John 20:26–29.

3 **Awareness** The Practice of Seeking

22 *Look, here* John 1:35–38.

23 *Ask* Matthew 7:7–8.

4 **What Do I *Really* Want?**
The Practice of Feeding Our Deepest Human Hungers

26 *I went* Henry David Thoreau, *Walden* (Boston: Shambhala, 2004), 77.

We must learn Thoreau, *Walden*, 77, 81.

27 *Children* Thoreau, *Walden*, 81.

28 *I have food* John 4:1–34.

I am the bread John 6:35.

29 *One does not* Matthew 4:4.

Blessed Matthew 5:6, Luke 6:21.

5 **Living Fully in the Moment** The Practice of Presence

33 *While washing* Thich Nhat Hanh, "The Miracle of Mindfulness," in *The Wisdom of Thich Nhat Hanh* (New York: Book-of-the-Month Club, 2000), 3–4.

That's precisely Thich Nhat Hanh, "The Miracle of Mindfulness," 4.

34 *People* Thich Nhat Hanh, "The Miracle of Mindfulness," 12.

The Holy Spirit Robert Ellsberg, *All Saints: Daily Reflections on Saints, Prophets, and Witnesses for Our Time* (New York: Crossroad, 1997), 104.

35 *What most* From "The Road to Daybreak," in *Seeds of Hope: A Henri Nouwen Reader*, ed. Robert Durback (New York: Doubleday, 1997), 54.

6 **Loneliness vs. Being Alone** The Practice of Solitude

43   *Before he began*   Matthew 4:1–11.

44   *Get up*   Matthew 26:36–46.

Loneliness   Richard J. Foster, *Celebration of Discipline: The Path to Spiritual Growth* (San Francisco: HarperSanFrancisco, 1998), 96. Originally published in 1978, this book is a classic on the spiritual disciplines and has sold more than a million copies.

7 **Companions on the Journey** The Practice of Friendship

47   *If we're really*   From the book Joanne Rogers helped assemble, titled *Life's Journeys According to Mister Rogers: Things to Remember Along the Way* (New York: Hyperion, 2005), 22–23.

49   *Likewise*   Matthew 19:19; John 15:12, emphasis mine.

It means befriending   Paul Wadell, *Friendship and the Moral Life* (Notre Dame, IN: University of Notre Dame Press, 1989), 73–74. Also see Waddell's chapter "What Medieval Monks Can Do For Us: Aelred of Rievaulx and the Life of Spiritual Friendship," in *Becoming Friends: Worship, Justice, and the Practice of Christian Friendship* (Grand Rapids, MI: Brazos Press, 2002).

50   *A recent study*   Liz Spencer and Ray Pahl, *Rethinking Friendship: Hidden Solidarities Today* (Princeton, NJ: Princeton University Press, 2006), 57–115. I am grateful to my friends, Karl and Michelle Clifton-Soderstrom, for recommending this book to me following a rich conversation about the nature of friendship as I worked on this chapter.

Confide, provide emotional support   Spencer and Pahl, *Rethinking Friendship*, 69.

8 **Spiritual Exercise** The Practice of Practice

54   *Train yourself*   1 Timothy 4:7–10.

A farmer   Foster, *Celebration of Discipline*, 7.

TWO **ROOTS**

9 Listening for the Still Small Voice of God
The Practice of Meditation

65   *Christian meditation*   Foster, *Celebration of Discipline*, 17.

66   *I will call*   Psalm 77:11–14.

    withdrew … to a   Matthew 14:13; Luke 6:12.

67   *come away*   Mark 6:31.

    to descend   As quoted in Foster, *Celebration of Discipline*, 19.

68   *rest in God*   For a concise and helpful overview of Benedictine spirituality and the practice of *lectio divina,* see Katherine Kraft, OSB, "Benedictine Spirituality: A Way of Living for God, Others, and the World," in *As Leaven in the World: Catholic Perspectives on Faith, Vocation, and the Intellectual Life,* ed. Thomas M. Landy (Franklin, WI: Sheed & Ward, 2001), 255–271.

69   *I simply followed*   Emilie Griffin, *Simple Ways to Pray: Spiritual Life in the Catholic Tradition* (Lanham, MD: Sheed & Ward, 2006), 124.

    when I couldn't   Griffin, *Simple Ways to Pray*, 125.

    in contemplative   Griffin, *Simple Ways to Pray*, 128.

70   *Meditation*   Thomas Merton, *Contemplative Prayer* (Garden City, NY: Doubleday, 1969), 39.

    In his book   Richard J. Foster, *Streams of Living Water: Celebrating the Great Traditions of Christian Faith* (San Francisco: HarperSanFrancisco, 1998), 56–58.

71   Katherine Kraft, OSB, "Benedictine Spirituality: A Way of Living for God, Others, and the World," in *As Leaven in the World,* 261.

73   *Practicing Lectio Divina*   Kraft, "Benedictine Spirituality," 262.

10 Lord, Teach Us to Pray The Practice of Prayer

75 *They felt something* Wayne Muller, *Learning to Pray: How We Find Heaven on Earth* (New York: Bantam Dell, 2003), 5.

Lord, teach us Luke 11:1–4; Matthew 6:9–13.

76 *Every day* Muller, *Learning to Pray*, 2.

80 *Be still* Psalm 46:10.

81 *The fruit* Galatians 5:22–23.

As a spiritual discipline For an excellent resource on prayer, see Emilie Griffin, *Simple Ways to Pray*.

11 Faith Seeking Understanding The Practice of Thinking

84 *One of the scientists* Alan Cooperman, "Researchers Break Ice on Jesus 'Miracle,'" *Washington Post,* April 6, 2006, A03.

85 *This isn't going* Cooperman, "Researchers Break Ice on Jesus 'Miracle.'"

87 *grappling with* James Turner, as quoted in Richard T. Hughes, *How Christian Faith Can Sustain the Life of the Mind* (Grand Rapids, MI: W.B. Eerdmans, 2001), 60.

And it emphasizes Hughes, *How Christian Faith Can Sustain the Life of the Mind*, 59–66.

In his book Foster, *Celebration of Discipline,* 64–66.

90 *There are certain* C.S. Lewis, *Mere Christianity* (New York: Macmillan, Collier Books, 1943), 126.

12 Touchstones of the Sacred
The Practice of Living Sacramentally

92 *A sacrament* Frederick Buechner, *Wishful Thinking: A Seeker's ABC* (San Francisco: HarperSanFrancisco, 1993), 101.

In other words Buechner, *Wishful Thinking,* 101.

94   *I focus*   Andre Dubus, "Sacraments," in *Meditations from a Movable Chair: Essays* (New York: Knopf, 1998), 85–90.

   Dubus goes on   Dubus, "Sacraments."

95   *Richard Foster*   Foster, *Streams of Living Water*, 266–70.

13 Marching with the Saints The Practice of Being Fully Alive

99   *Knowing this*   James Martin, SJ, *My Life with the Saints* (Chicago: Loyola Press, 2006), 7–8.

100   *Jim*   I'm forever grateful to Jim for introducing me to another saint—my wife, Liz, whom he knew in graduate school at Weston Jesuit School of Theology before she moved to Chicago for her PhD at Loyola University.

104   *As Dorothy Day*   Ellsberg, *All Saints*, 2.

14 Where Am I Going, and How Do I Get There?
The Practice of Spiritual Direction

108   *A three-year-old girl*   Marcus Borg, *The Heart Of Christianity: Rediscovering a Life of Faith* (San Francisco: HarperSanFrancisco, 2003), 113–114.

THREE BRANCHES

Introduction

116   *I am the true*   John 15:1–10.

117   *Paul teaches*   Galatians 5:22–23.

15 How, Then, Shall I Live? The Practice of Vocation

119   *My question*   Leo Tolstoy, *Confession,* trans. David Patterson (New York: Norton, 1983), 34. Tolstoy's original work was written in 1879. Having published two masterworks, *War and Peace* and *Anna Karenina,* Tolstoy experienced a spiritual crisis in which he sought

to know God and understand the meaning of life. Like his novels, Tolstoy's *Confession* is a great literary work that probes the deepest questions of life.

120 *Because we spend* Al Gini, *My Job, My Self: Work and the Creation of the Modern Individual* (New York: Routledge, 2000), ix, 2.

122 *By coming* Parker Palmer, *Let Your Life Speak: Listening for the Voice of Vocation* (San Francisco: Jossey-Bass, 2000), 9.

Before Palmer, *Let Your Life Speak*, 4–5.

123 *I came* John 10:10.

16 See How They Love One Another The Practice of Community

125 *The basic* L'Arche is an international network of more than one hundred communities in thirty countries for people with intellectual disabilities. Henri Nouwen served as senior pastor of l'Arche Daybreak in Toronto, Canada.

In the parable Luke 10:25–37.

128 *When he learned* John 11:43–44.

Father, forgive Luke 23:34.

Put your finger John 20:27.

130 *We remember* Robert Schreiter, cpps, *The Ministry of Reconciliation: Spirituality and Strategies* (Maryknoll, NY: Orbis Books, 1998), 66–67.

Do not judge Luke 6:37.

17 How Do I Get Free? How Do I Stay Free?
The Practice of Letting Go

135 *I came* John 10:10.

136 *He simply* *The Way of a Pilgrim,* trans. Helen Bacovcin (New York: Doubleday, 1992), 13.

137–38 *Make time* *The Way of a Pilgrim*, 194.

ABOUT **PARACLETE PRESS**

Who We Are

Paraclete Press is an ecumenical publisher of books and recordings on Christian spirituality. Our publishing represents a full expression of Christian belief and practice—from Catholic to Evangelical, from Protestant to Orthodox.

Paraclete Press is the publishing arm of the Community of Jesus, an ecumenical monastic community in the Benedictine tradition. As such, we are uniquely positioned in the marketplace without connection to a large corporation and with informal relationships to many branches and denominations of faith.

We like it best when people buy our books from booksellers, our partners in successfully reaching as wide an audience as possible.

What We Are Doing

Books Paraclete Press publishes books that show the richness and depth of what it means to be Christian. Although Benedictine spirituality is at the heart of all that we do, we publish books that reflect the Christian experience across many cultures, time periods, and houses of worship.

We publish books that nourish the vibrant life of the church and its people—books about spiritual practice, formation, history, ideas, and customs.

We have several different series of books within Paraclete Press, including the best-selling Living Library series of modernized classic texts; A Voice from the Monastery—giving voice to men and women monastics about what it means to live a spiritual life today; award-winning literary faith fiction; and books that explore Judaism and Islam and discover how these faiths inform Christian thought and practice.

Recordings From Gregorian chant to contemporary American choral works, our music recordings celebrate the richness of sacred choral music through the centuries. Paraclete is proud to distribute the recordings of the internationally acclaimed choir Gloriæ Dei Cantores, who have been praised for their "rapt and fathomless spiritual intensity" by *American Record Guide,* and the Gloriæ Dei Cantores Schola, which specializes in the study and performance of Gregorian chant. Paraclete is also the exclusive North American distributor of the recordings of the Monastic Choir of St. Peter's Abbey in Solesmes, France, long considered to be a leading authority on Gregorian chant performance.

Learn more about us at our Web site: www.paracletepress.com, or call us toll-free at 1-800-451-5006.

ALSO RECOMMENDED

The Way of Mary
Following Her Footsteps Toward God

ISBN: 978-1-55725-522-8 | Price: $19.95 | Hardcover, 180 pages

Visiting a remote village in Guatemala, Mary Ford–Grabowsky encountered a Mayan statue of the Virgin Mary. Although she had experienced many wondrous moments in her life as a spiritual teacher, the depths of love she sensed in this small chapel surpassed them all. Ford-Grabowsky set out to discover all she could about Mary, and to find new ways of relating to the woman who has had such a momentous influence on history and the human heart.

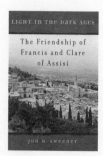

Light in the Dark Ages
The Friendship of Francis and Clare of Assisi

ISBN: 978-1-55725-476-4 | Price: $16.95 | Paperback, 224 pages

The Middle Ages were not so very dark, as the old textbooks say. As you will discover in this intriguing portrait of the first Franciscans, we live in dark ages whenever we become preoccupied with power. In this popular history, Jon Sweeney reveals the timeless temptations that come with being human—greed, competition, ego, and selfishness—as well as the many ways that Francis and Clare of Assisi inspired change and brought light into darkness.